Supporting Indigenous Students to Succeed at University

I0130372

Addressing a significant gap in the literature, this book provides conceptual and practical foundations for the development of more effective support strategies to improve academic outcomes for Indigenous higher education students.

Authors Martin and Vicky Nakata draw on Indigenous and higher education research, as well as their own experience implementing reforms to Indigenous student support services in Australian universities, to present a method that focuses on helping students to develop the skills and capabilities they need to thrive at university. The book is divided into three sections, the first outlining fifteen key concepts and conditions for student success. The second section provides detailed guidance on individual student case management, from foundational concepts through to implementation. The third section outlines what staff need to consider before attempting to implement changes to practice in their local context, offering a blueprint for assessing current practice, planning for and then implementing change.

Presenting an approach that has proven successful in closing the gap between the academic outcomes of Indigenous and non-Indigenous students, this book is an essential resource for academic and non-academic staff who support underprepared students to succeed in higher education.

Martin Nakata is the Deputy Vice-Chancellor of Indigenous Education & Strategy and Head of the Indigenous Education and Research Centre at James Cook University.

Vicky Nakata, now retired, was a Researcher in the Indigenous Education and Research Centre at James Cook University.

Supporting Indigenous Students to Succeed at University

A Resource for the Higher Education Sector

Martin Nakata and Vicky Nakata

Routledge
Taylor & Francis Group

LONDON AND NEW YORK

Cover image: © Getty Images

First published 2023
by Routledge
4 Park Square, Milton Park, Abingdon, Oxon OX14 4RN

and by Routledge
605 Third Avenue, New York, NY 10158

Routledge is an imprint of the Taylor & Francis Group, an informa business

British Library Cataloguing-in-Publication Data
A catalogue record for this book is available from the British Library

ISBN: 978-1-032-35348-7 (hbk)
ISBN: 978-1-032-35346-3 (pbk)
ISBN: 978-1-003-32645-8 (ebk)

DOI: 10.4324/9781003326458

Typeset in Bembo
by SPi Technologies India Pvt Ltd (Straive)

This book is dedicated to all the Indigenous and non-Indigenous students who willingly gave their time to be interviewed over a three-year period as part of an Australian Research Council study on Indigenous academic persistence. Your insights and reflections on your learning journeys have been invaluable and have helped inform the direction and contents of this book.

Contents

Figures

Acknowledgements

We would like to acknowledge the Australian Research Council who funded the study into the academic persistence of Indigenous higher education students that led to this book and the contributions of our research collaborators, Professor Andy Day and Dr Gregory Martin.

We would also like to acknowledge and thank the Indigenous support managers and support staff of the three Indigenous support units that gave their time, knowledge, experience, and support to the study and for their continued interest and collaboration through annual symposiums as critical friends. Particular thanks go to Mr Mick Peachey, Ms Cheryl Ah-See, Professor Yvonne Cadet-James, Professor Braden Hill, and Professor Chanelle van den Berg.

We also gratefully acknowledge and thank the support staff in the two Indigenous support units with whom we worked closely for their commitment and efforts during the implementation of new services, systems, processes, and strategies. A special acknowledgement as well to our industry partners Kevin Hemmett and Eric Schwantler from WillowSoft Student Success Platform.

Acronyms

GPA   Grade Point Average
IEU   Indigenous Education Unit
ILSP   Indigenous Learning Support Plan
PELA   Pre Entry Language Assessment
STEM Science, Technology, Engineering, Mathematics
TAFE Technical and Further Education

Introduction

Background

Historical educational disadvantage and continuing low schooling outcomes restrict the ability of many Indigenous people to access, participate, and succeed in higher education studies. Many of those who gain entry to university experience a range of challenges that threaten their chances of success.[1] These challenges can be categorised into three principal areas:

- challenges associated with the mastery and performance of academic knowledge and skills to meet academic expectations and demands
- challenges associated with Indigenous students' interactions in the teaching and learning and social and administrative environments of universities
- challenges associated with a range of external, personal, and cultural factors, such as finance and accommodation, cultural dislocation, and challenges related to health, disability, socio-emotional wellbeing and family, work, and community responsibilities.[2]

Difficulties in any of these areas can affect a student's ability to persist and succeed. However, challenges for Indigenous students often occur across all these areas and can occur at any time during a student's journey through university studies.

Over decades, the Indigenous higher education sector has been active in its efforts to remove the institutional barriers to Indigenous people's access, participation, and success in higher education and has developed an extensive agenda for achieving this.[3] This agenda aligns with a wider debate in the higher education sector about the degree to which universities should adjust their practices in response to the diversity of their student populations and the degree to which students from diverse backgrounds should be expected to integrate and adjust to traditional university demands and expectations.[4] For the Indigenous higher education sector, the accommodation of Indigenous concerns by universities is not just an equity and inclusion issue but a matter of social justice and reconciliation.

The Indigenous higher education sector's institutional change agenda is broad and includes attention to access conditions and enabling pathways; Indigenous student support provisions, including funding and student financial assistance programs; the inclusion and treatment of Indigenous content in curricula; academic

DOI: 10.4324/9781003326458-1

teaching and learning practices; impediments to access and participation in particular disciplines, for example, STEM areas; the social and classroom environments in universities; student services and administration practices; the cultural competence of university staff, students, and graduates; employment levels and conditions of both Indigenous academics and Indigenous general staff in universities; Indigenous research and postgraduate research student issues; the need for a whole-of-university effort to improve Indigenous outcomes; and Indigenous university policies and governance issues.[5] This has been a sustained and generally effective agenda, considering the many barriers that have had to be persistently challenged over decades.

Indigenous student support units were the first area of institutional change Indigenous people achieved, and they have operated in Australian universities for three to four decades, beginning in the former Colleges of Advanced Education before their amalgamation with the university sector.[6] These student support units have been credited with the successes of Indigenous students, and until recently, they were not held accountable for low student outcomes in recognition of the many barriers that Indigenous people face.[7] Nationally, Indigenous student outcomes continue to be comparatively lower than non-Indigenous student outcomes, although it is important to highlight that Indigenous student outcomes are uneven across the nation's universities.[8]

Regarding student success, the 2012 *Review of Higher Education, Access and Outcomes for Aboriginal and Torres Strait Islander People Final Report* (the Review) expressed concerns about the marginalisation of Indigenous support units within universities, the skill levels of Indigenous support staff, and the effectiveness of Indigenous support practices.[9] It recommended distributing the responsibilities for Indigenous student academic and pastoral support across the faculties, university student services divisions, and Indigenous education units (IEU) as part of a shift to a whole-of-university responsibility and effort to improve Indigenous outcomes.[10] Since then, individual universities have followed these recommendations to varying degrees. In some universities, Indigenous student support continues to be entirely run by IEUs, with pro-vice-chancellors or other senior Indigenous staff directing the broader institutional changes across the university. Other universities have shifted academic support to faculties but left pastoral and cultural support and the administration of supplementary tutorial programs in IEUs; at least one university has redistributed all Indigenous support services across the university.[11]

Redistributing the responsibilities for student support across the university does not necessarily lead to more effective support practices or more efficient delivery of services. Conversely, leaving student support strategies unchanged in IEUs, especially in those universities with low Indigenous student outcomes, does not necessarily achieve this either. It is the case that whatever a university's preferred model for Indigenous student support services, improving Indigenous student support services does require across-university relationships and cooperative, whole-of-university efforts.[12] It also now requires cooperation between Indigenous and non-Indigenous staff in different sections of the university and between senior Indigenous staff and Indigenous student support managers and staff.[13] Most importantly, it requires attention to the day-to-day work and support strategies that constitute support staff practices.

However, since the Review and amidst the Indigenous efforts to establish broader institutional change in universities, less attention has been given to the effectiveness of the day-to-day work of Indigenous student support staff. These staff are responsible for the practical efforts to deliver effective support to students who need it to overcome their challenges and increase their chances of success. Close attention must be given to the actual work of student support to improve Indigenous students' educational outcomes—that is, to considering what support services and interventions are indicated for different disciplinary cohorts and individual students; what sorts of support staff strategies, practices, and systems are needed to deliver them; and what sort of adjustments to current services and strategies might be indicated by a university's Indigenous student outcomes. Improvements to the way student support is conducted need to be considered within the specific contexts of each university, as the Review stated.[14] However, this raises the following questions: What sort of information or guidance is available to assist Indigenous student support staff in each university to improve the effectiveness of their support services? On what basis should they determine what needs to change and what will improve practices?

The factors that affect Indigenous student higher education outcomes are well-known across the sector, have been well documented in the Indigenous higher education literature for more than three decades, and have been consistently reported anecdotally over time.[15] However, less sustained attention has been given to the efficacy of day-to-day Indigenous student support practices in the literature. While a segment of the Indigenous higher education literature has always focused on Indigenous student support practices and continues to focus on them, overall, the attention in this area has been intermittent and scattered across time and different university contexts, disciplines, or stages of the educational journey.[16] During the last decade, propositions for lifting Indigenous higher education student outcomes have included requests for more attention to Indigenous student finances, enabling pathways, tracking and monitoring Indigenous student progress, and more effective support strategies and interventions.[17] Some recent literature has also explored some key concepts associated with learning and success, access, transition and enabling pathways, and whole-of-university efforts.[18]

In addition to the Indigenous higher education student support literature, there is a vast higher education literature for the Indigenous support sector to draw on.[19] Generally, this literature explores institutional efforts to improve all students' transition, retention, success, academic learning, and university experiences. This is an international, scholarly, and quite complex research field for support staff to traverse and process for practical strategies or implications for their own practices. The literature has accumulated over time, draws on a range of disciplines and theoretical perspectives, explores a range of overlapping and interrelated academic concepts, and largely reports on specific empirical studies related to these.[20]

From our observations over decades, a dissemination gap exists between the relevant academic literature and the Indigenous student support workforce, particularly the pastoral support staff, who, in many cases, have not fully understood the academic demands placed on students. Support staff have little time to keep abreast of relevant literature, let alone reflect on its implications for their own work. For obvious and practical reasons, the focus of Indigenous student support staff is on Indigenous students and the issues for which they require immediate assistance on a day-to-day basis.

While Indigenous student experience studies and reports of practical support strategies attempt to bridge this dissemination gap, in our experience, most Indigenous support staff tend not to engage the literature directly but rely on their own accumulated understandings of the Indigenous students' journey and experiences. These are largely derived from the circulating Indigenous higher education discourse (which may include ideas, concepts, or trends from the academic discourse regarding student success and student support); established Indigenous support practices; support managers' visions and directives or, in the absence of these, staff members' initiatives; staff members' knowledge, beliefs, assumptions, and experiences of higher education, their students, and their students' needs and responsibilities; and Indigenous community views about the purposes of higher education for Indigenous people and what it should prioritise and deliver to Indigenous students. National Indigenous student support sector networks are also key sites for student support staff to share challenges, strategies, concerns, and grievances about university practices, students, and support provisions.[21] However, these national conversations often lead to requests for changes to institutional practices and/or government funding program conditions to address common concerns rather than methods for improving the efficacy of day-to-day support strategies in specific contexts.

This is not to suggest that there is not a useful and relevant Indigenous and higher education student support literature to inform changes to Indigenous support practices or that higher-level Indigenous strategies, academic research, and practical changes from Indigenous student support staff have not been ongoing over time in different universities to improve the effectiveness of Indigenous student support practices. It also does not suggest that Indigenous support strategies, as they are, do not assist students to succeed; there is ample evidence they do for many students. Rather, it emphasises that there has been no comprehensive, focused, educationally informed guidance for the Indigenous student support sector in Australian universities.

This is particularly unhelpful for those who want to improve the effectiveness of their services but who need more knowledge and information to do so, or for those on the ground who work in situations without effective and educationally informed leadership. Knowledge and informed leadership are essential to beginning the processes involved in reviewing, reflecting on, and changing or adjusting support approaches and practices to be more effective or serve more students. There is also a lack of aligned practical guidance for efficiently delivering such services to large and diverse cohorts of Indigenous students. Efficient delivery of services requires the development of efficient systems and processes. This is an unhelpful situation for Indigenous support managers and frontline personnel who, considering the current national performance funding model, are now under pressure to account for their efforts to improve student outcomes, alongside the university as a whole.[22]

Given this situation, from what basis will Indigenous support managers and staff instigate changes in their own universities that will lead to more effective practices?

In the context of higher-level, whole-of-university Indigenous strategies, policies, and governance, how are Indigenous student support managers or staff to advocate effectively for changes they might want to trial or implement if these have implications for resources, funding, or other areas of the university?

In the national conversation about Indigenous students' needs, the broader Indigenous focus on dismantling systemic barriers and ensuring whole-of-university efforts and responsibility for Indigenous student outcomes has taken the focus away from how student support is actually conducted. This is despite the post-Review work that has been done in the enabling access, pathways, and transition areas and the commitment expressed by Universities Australia in its Indigenous strategies and annual reports.[23] In the current era, Indigenous support managers need to be able to articulate an informed basis for mounting persuasive arguments for changed arrangements, especially those likely to involve significant reorganisation or development of services or resources, to influence Indigenous or other senior staff. Similarly, both student support managers and staff need to be able to argue from an informed position if they strongly disagree with student support change proposals. Indigenous student support managers also need to present an informed change argument to their student support team and guide any change processes, including any indicated need for professional development. Staff also need to have a sound basis for their suggestions to managers about any changes or adjustments to practices.

Arguments for changes to staff practices are strengthened if informed by a range of knowledge sets concerning Indigenous student outcomes within a university, what is expected of students if they are to succeed in learning, the capabilities students need to be successful learners, students' actual capacities and circumstances, the barriers and enablers of success, how universities work, and, for managers, knowledge about shifting policies and funding arrangements. Despite this need for relevant knowledge, there has been little emphasis on the professional development of Indigenous student support staff beyond the normal apprentice and induction approaches involved with learning on the job and the professional development associated with using university systems and compliance with university policies.[24]

Any attempt to establish changes to student support practices involves many detailed considerations before a strategically planned approach to change can be developed. A range of questions must be considered: Why do things need to change? What needs to change? How is that to be determined? What has to be thought about when considering changes? What strategies need review and development to be more responsive to student needs? What ideas, thinking, or evidence should support strategies and practices be based on? How is a relatively small number of support staff to understand and provide for the individual needs of large cohorts of students? What changes to systems and processes are needed to implement strategies to enable more efficient practices? What should support staff do on an annual, semester, weekly, and daily basis to increase Indigenous students' chances of success? What are the minimum levels of knowledge about higher education learning and university systems and processes that support staff need to be more effective? How will the effectiveness of strategies and practices be evaluated to inform ongoing improvements? What are the implications of any changes for staffing, staff roles, and budgets? How should Indigenous values and priorities be upheld? What are the ethical implications of any changes to practices, such as for students' privacy and confidentiality? This book aims to address these questions and concerns.

About the book

This book has been written primarily for the Indigenous higher education student support sector in Australia. It aims to assist Indigenous student support managers and staff in their efforts to improve Indigenous support services and practices in their own universities. The intention is to facilitate a process for change that can be driven, managed, and implemented by Indigenous student support managers and their staff, albeit with backup from senior Indigenous staff and others in universities. The book should also be informative for senior university staff and interested academics and university program managers who do not always understand what Indigenous student support staff do or the challenges they face in delivering effective support to Indigenous students. More broadly, it should be of interest to anyone involved in supporting underprepared university or tertiary-level students.

The book addresses what needs to be considered in any plan to improve the effectiveness and efficiency of Indigenous student support services and practices. The contents are directed towards the educational goal of improving the success, progression, and completion rates of Indigenous students in a university in a way that enables students to develop the range of capabilities they need to function successfully and eventually independently in their courses.

The book fills a gap in the Indigenous student support literature by emphasising key educational concepts and influences related to higher education learning and academic success. This emphasis aims to deepen Indigenous student support staff knowledge and understanding of what is involved in the students' efforts to become successful and independent learners. Many of these concepts circulate as part of the support discourse, but their meaning and implications for academic outcomes are not well understood. Explorations of key concepts support the central concern of the book, which is the need to understand Indigenous students primarily as learners who must 'learn how to learn' in higher education, at the same time as attending to the gaps in the prerequisite academic knowledge on which their academic learning in their subjects is based. The intention of this emphasis is to supplement the knowledge and experience that Indigenous student support staff have accumulated over decades in the provision of pastoral (personal, social, and cultural) support for Indigenous students. Together, these sets of knowledge and experience provide a more informed basis for thinking about the 'why, what, and how' of any changes to Indigenous support provisions, systems, processes, strategies, and practices to ensure students develop the capacities required to become progressively more independent and in control of their learning.

The focus on developing student capabilities should not be wrongly interpreted as placing the burden of responsibility for success onto students rather than on the range of systemic barriers they confront in and out of the university. On the contrary, most of the key concepts discussed in this book stress the complex interplay between students' own capacities and attributes, institutional environment factors, and external factors associated with students' circumstances. The complex interactions between many variables often mean that students' academic and pastoral support needs are not always entirely separable and that academic and pastoral support staff must work closely together to support students as they develop the capabilities needed for success. This is particularly critical for academically and socially underprepared students, culturally uncomfortable or alienated students, or students with complex life circumstances. These students need well-coordinated or integrated academic and pastoral support. Such students constitute a large majority of the national Indigenous student cohort and the entire Indigenous cohort in some universities.

Similarly, this focus does not in any way detract from the importance of the ongoing Indigenous institutional change agenda or the need for universities to take more responsibility for the whole-of-university approach to improving Indigenous higher education outcomes. Rather, it suggests that despite being present in universities for more than three decades, the Indigenous student support workforce has been quite neglected regarding professional development relevant to the effectiveness and efficiencies of their day-to-day work practices. For this reason, the contents of this book are directed towards the knowledge base and service delivery issues encountered by Indigenous student support managers and staff and not the wider concerns of the Indigenous institutional change agenda or the politics and scholarly debates within Indigenous higher education.[25]

In the university ecosystem, Indigenous student support practices should currently be considered part of the institutional environmental factors that influence Indigenous student success. Indigenous student support services exist to assist students in overcoming any obstacles, negative influences, and gaps in the knowledge, strategies, and skills they need to succeed and eventually be able to learn with minimal support. It is important that the Indigenous student support workforce is appropriately informed, resourced, skilled, and confident in their ability to provide the indicated levels of support to all Indigenous students who need support to succeed. Therefore, this book emphasises the potential areas for improvement that are within the control of support staff and some of the more difficult areas of change that will require managers to stimulate discussions and actions in Indigenous policy and strategy arenas and other areas of the university.

It is also important to understand that this book is only a guide to the issues that need to be considered when making decisions to improve support provisions, strategies, and practices. It is not a prescription for practice because there is no one way to provide effective and efficient support to fit the specific Indigenous student and cohort needs and contexts of all universities. The decisions and planning involved in improving support services, strategies, and practices must be developed in the local context of each university and in relation to its Indigenous student cohort and their needs. This book has set about providing a more informed basis from which to do so.

Although this book is presented as a resource or reference for those wanting to improve their practices, we suggest that Indigenous student support managers and staff initially read all chapters in sequence. This will enable a fuller understanding of the shift towards a primary focus on Indigenous students as learners and an approach to student support that focuses on developing the capabilities students require to succeed. After an initial read-through, staff can revisit sections as needed when trying to understand or respond to students' issues and needs or planning strategies or processes. We emphasise that the contents are only a starting point for thinking about changes to Indigenous student support approaches and practices. The real work must be done in context and on the ground over time.

The book is divided into three chapters. Chapter 1 explores key concepts and study conditions that influence student success and provides essential background knowledge for managers and staff about higher education learning and student effort. The fields of relevant research that we have accessed are vast, complex, and debated; however, we have attempted to make key understandings as accessible as possible without entering any debates or the full literature. While Chapter 1 is lengthy, we emphasise that there is no requirement to master or recall all the details of these discussions. It is included to be kept in mind or referred back to when trying to understand students' challenges and where they feel stuck.

Chapters 2 and 3 build from these foundations to examine the more practical 'what and how' issues and practices that support managers and staff might need to audit and consider when making changes or adjustments to their current support approaches. Chapter 2 discusses the essential elements of an effective individual student case management system and other issues that need to be considered to develop students' capacities to succeed. Assisting staff to monitor and track students' needs, student progress, and the staff interventions undertaken to assist students is an important part of a case management system. Chapter 3 discusses broader issues that need to be considered by managers to support the implementation of a student capacity development approach and also includes more discussion of some elements of individual student case management. We conclude the book by summarising the key points we have found to be critical to building more effective support practices.

The book does not focus on support for postgraduate students. Although much of this book can be applied to supporting students undertaking postgraduate coursework programs, support for Indigenous higher degrees by research students requires a different discussion and strategy. This does not suggest that Indigenous education units have nothing to offer in the way of support for higher degrees by research students; they should offer assistance if they can or at least know whom to refer students to for assistance.

The book is an applied outcome of an earlier Australian Research Council project investigation into Indigenous students' academic persistence.[26] As part of this project, Indigenous and non-Indigenous students from three universities across three states in Australia were interviewed over one to three years, from 2014 to 2016. These interviews focused on the nature of students' learning challenges and what they did when they encountered a learning challenge. Insights from these interviews led to further exploration, beyond the Indigenous higher education literature, of key educational concepts and influences on student success and resulted in the focus we have placed on understanding Indigenous students as learners. In places, students' insights have been included where relevant to add to the discussion.

Use of terms

Throughout this book, the term 'Indigenous' is used for shorthand purposes to mean Aboriginal and Torres Strait Islander people. We use separate terms 'Aboriginal' or 'Torres Strait Islander' when discussing only one of these groups, citing literature that uses that terminology or where it is more appropriate to the discussion.

Similarly, 'students' can be assumed to refer to Indigenous students unless preceded by 'other,' 'non-Indigenous,' or 'Australian' students or the inclusive 'all students.' The terminology of 'student services' or 'university student services' can be assumed to mean the standard university array of student services offered to all students, not Indigenous student support services or any other specialised Indigenous student services in the university.

The term 'Indigenous student support staff' includes all staff who support Indigenous students, whether Indigenous or non-Indigenous, though most support staff in Australian universities are Aboriginal and Torres Strait Islander people.

The terms 'subjects' and 'courses' refer to units of study and enabling, preparation, or degree programs for universities, respectively. We note that this terminology is not standard across the country and that many universities refer to subjects as 'courses' and courses as 'programs.'

The terms 'capacities,' 'abilities,' and 'capabilities' are used interchangeably. While these terms are accepted as synonyms in their general use, we acknowledge there are sometimes particular distinctions in meanings applied in some areas of academic scholarship. These distinctions mainly appear to concern the difference between a person's existing and potential ability and the contexts in which the terms are used to indicate a specific meaning.

We use the term 'IEU' (Indigenous Education Unit) to refer to Indigenous student support centres. Some IEUs combine Indigenous Studies teaching, Indigenous research, and student support units. Some universities have standalone Indigenous student support units.

Notes

1 Behrendt et al., 2012.
2 See the Indigenous higher education literature relating to students, e.g., Barney, 2016; Behrendt et al., 2012; Bourke et al., 1996; Burden et al., 1998; Hearn et al., 2019; Nakata et al., 2008; Oliver et al., 2013a, 2013b, 2016; Rigney & Neill, 2018; Schwartz, 2018; Taylor et al., 2019; Usher et al., 2005.
3 See, e.g., Behrendt et al., 2012; National Indigenous Higher Education Advisory Council (IHEAC), 2006, 2011. See also the National Aboriginal & Torres Strait Islander Higher Education Consortium's website (https://natsihec.edu.au/).
4 See, e.g., Zepke & Leach, 2005.
5 See, e.g., Asmar, 2014a, 2014b; Australian Council of Graduate Research, n.d.; Behrendt et al., 2012; IHEAC, 2006, 2011; Universities Australia, 2011.
6 Bin-Sallik, 1990.
7 See Behrendt et al., 2012.
8 Pechenkina & Anderson, 2011.
9 See Behrendt et al., 2012.

10 Behrendt et al., 2012, p. xix, Recommendation 10.
11 See Asmar & Page, 2017.
12 See Behrendt et al., 2012.
13 For an example of developing a whole-of-university approach, see Uink et al., 2019; for a whole-of-school/disciplinary cohort approach, see Fowler et al., 2018.
14 Behrendt et al., 2012, p. 63.
15 See, e.g., Barney, 2016; Bourke et al., 1996; Malcolm & Rochecouste, 2002; Oliver et al., 2016; Page et al., 1997; Rigney & Neill, 2018; Taylor et al., 2019; Usher et al., 2005.
16 See, e.g., Foley, 1996; Fredericks et al., 2015b; Hearn et al., 2019; Nakata et al., 2008; Schulz et al., 2018; Schwartz, 2018.
17 See, e.g., Behrendt et al., 2012; Fredericks et al., 2015a; Nakata, 2013.
18 See, e.g., Buckskin et al., 2018; Frawley et al., 2017b; Kinnane et al., 2014; Uink et al., 2019.
19 See, e.g., Kinnane, et al., 2014.
20 For an example of an overview of research approaches, see Kuh et al., 2006.
21 See, e.g., the National Aboriginal & Torres Strait Islander Higher Education Consortium (previously National Indigenous Higher Education Network) website (https://natsihec.edu.au/).
22 See Universities Australia, 2017; see also National Indigenous Australians Agency, Indigenous Student Success Program (n.d.).
23 See, e.g., Fredericks et al., 2015a; Frawley et al., 2017a; Kinnane et al., 2014; Universities Australia, 2017, 2019, 2020.
24 See Nakata et al., 2008.
25 Includes both Indigenous and non-Indigenous staff who support Indigenous students.
26 See Day et al., 2015; Nakata et al., 2019a, 2019b.

References

Asmar, C. (2014a). *Indigenous teaching at Australian universities: Research-based approaches to teaching Indigenous students and Indigenous curriculum.* Australian Government Office for Learning and Teaching. http://www.indigenousteaching.com/indigenous-teaching-australian-universities

Asmar, C. (2014b). *Indigenous teaching at Australian universities: Research-based approaches to teaching Indigenous students and Indigenous curriculum.* Australian Government Office for Learning and Teaching. http://www.indigenousteaching.com/files/site/docs/10665-Murrup%20Barrak-Indigenous%20Teaching%20Booklet-FA-WEB.pdf

Asmar, C. & Page, S. (2017). Pigeonholed, peripheral or pioneering? Findings from a national study of Indigenous Australian academics in the disciplines. *Studies in Higher Education, 43*(9), 1679–1691. https://doi.org/10.1080/03075079.2017.1281240

Australian Council of Graduate Research. (n.d.). *ACGR good practice guidelines for Aboriginal and Torres Strait Islander research education.* https://www.acgr.edu.au/key-initiatives/indigenous-graduate-research/

Barney, K. (2016). Listening to and learning from the experiences of Aboriginal and Torres Strait Islander students to facilitate success. *Student Success, 7*(1), 1–11. https://doi.org/10.5204/ssj.v7i1.317

Behrendt, L., Larkin, S., Griew, R. & Kelly, P. (2012, July). *Review of higher education, access and outcomes for Aboriginal and Torres Strait Islander People final report.* Australian Government. https://www.dese.gov.au/aboriginal-and-torres-strait-islander-higher-education/review-higher-education-access-and-outcomes-aboriginal-and-torres-strait-islander-people

Bin-Sallik, M. A. (1990). *Aboriginal tertiary education in Australia.* University of South Australia, Aboriginal Studies Key Centre.

Bourke, C. J., Burden, J. K. & Moore, S. (1996). *Factors affecting the performance of Aboriginal and Torres Strait Islander students at Australian universities: A case study.* Australian Government Publishing Service.

Buckskin, P., Tranthim-Fryer, M., Holt, L., Gili, J., Heath, J., Smith, D., Larkin, S., Ireland, S., MacGibbon, L., Robertson, K., Small, T., Butler, K., Chatfield, T., Anderson, P. & Ma Rhea, Z. (2018, January). *Accelerating Indigenous higher education: Consultation paper.* National Aboriginal and Torres Strait Islander Higher Education Consortium. https://eprints.qut.edu.au/197728/1/NATSIHEC_%2BAIHE_FinaL_%2BReport%2BJan%2B2018_updated_031218.pdf

Burden, J., Bourke, E. A., Bourke, C. & Rigby, K. (1998). *Access, participation, transformation: A study of factors contributing to Indigenous student attrition and retention at University of Technology Sydney.* Aboriginal Research Institute, University of South Australia.

Day, A., Nakata, V., Nakata, M. & Martin, G. (2015). Indigenous students' persistence in higher education in Australia: Contextualising models of change from psychology to understand and aid students' practices at a cultural interface. *Higher Education Research & Development, 34*(3), 501–512. https://doi.org/10.1080/07294360.2014.973379

Foley, D. (1996). Perspectives on effective student support for Indigenous students in a tertiary institution. *Australian Journal of Indigenous Education, 24*(2), 53–55. https://doi.org/10.1017/S1326011100002477

Fowler, A. C., Ewens, B., Vafeas, C., Delves, L., Hayward, C., Nannup, N. & Baum, G. (2018). Closing the gap: A whole of school approach to Aboriginal and Torres Strait Islander inclusivity in higher education. *Nurse Education in Practice, 30*, 86–90. https://doi.org/10.1016/j.nepr.2018.04.001

Frawley, J., Larkin, S. & Smith, J. A. (Eds.). (2017a). *Indigenous pathways, transitions and participation in higher education: From policy to practice.* Springer Singapore.

Frawley, J., Ober, R., Olcay, M. & Smith, J. A. (2017b). *Indigenous achievement in higher education and the role of self-efficacy: Rippling stories of success.* National Centre for Student Equity in Higher Education. https://www.ncsehe.edu.au/wp-content/uploads/2017/05/Frawley_Rippling-Stories.pdf

Fredericks, B., Kinnear, S., Daniels, C., CroftWarcon, P. & Mann, J. (2015a). *Path+ways: Towards best practice in Indigenous access education.* National Centre for Student Equity in Higher Education. https://www.ncsehe.edu.au/publications/pathways-towards-best-practice-bridging-indigenous-participation-regional-dual-sector-universities/

Fredericks, B., Mann, J., Skinner, R., CroftWarcon, P. & McFarlane, B. (2015b). Enabling Indigenous education success beyond regional borders. *Journal of Economic and Social Policy, 17*(2), Article 31–14. https://eprints.qut.edu.au/91613/

Hearn, S., Benton, M., Funnell, S. & Marmolejo-Ramos, F. (2019). Investigation of the factors contributing to Indigenous students' retention and attrition rates at the University of Adelaide. *Australian Journal of Indigenous Education, 50*(1), 1–9. https://doi.org/10.1017/jie.2019.5

Kinnane, S., Wilks, J., Wilson, K., Hughes, T. & Thomas, S. (2014). *'Can't be what you can't see': The transition of Aboriginal and Torres Strait Islander students into higher education. Final report 2014.* The University of Notre Dame Australia. https://www.notredame.edu.au/__data/assets/pdf_file/0020/2882/SI11-2138-OLT-Final-Report-FINAL-Web.pdf

Kuh, G. D., Kinzie, J., Buckley, J. A., Bridges, B. K. & Hayek, J. C. (2006, July). *What matters to student success: A review of the literature. Commissioned report for the national symposium on postsecondary student success: Spearheading a dialog on student success.* National Postsecondary Education Cooperative. https://nces.ed.gov/npec/pdf/kuh_team_report.pdf

Malcolm, I. G. & Rochecouste, J. (2002, July). *Barriers to Indigenous student success in higher education* [Conference presentation]. *Higher Education Research and Development Society of Australasia Conference*, Perth, Western Australia.

Nakata, M. (2013). The rights and blights of the politics in Indigenous higher education. *Anthropological Forum*, *23*(3), 289–303. https://doi.org/10.1080/00664677.2013.803457

Nakata, M., Nakata, V. & Chin, M. (2008). Approaches to the academic support of Australian Indigenous students for tertiary studies. *Australian Journal of Indigenous Education*, *37*(S1), 137–145. https://doi.org/10.1375/S1326011100000478

Nakata, M., Nakata, V., Day, A., Martin, G. & Peachey, M. (2019a). Indigenous undergraduates' use of supplementary tutors: Developing academic capabilities for success in higher education studies. *Australian Journal of Indigenous Education*, *48*(2), 119–128. https://doi.org/10.1017/jie.2017.39

Nakata, M., Nakata, V., Day, A. & Peachey, M. (2019b). Closing gaps in Indigenous undergraduate higher education outcomes: Repositioning the role of student support services to improve retention and completion rates. *Australian Journal of Indigenous Education*, *48*(1), 1–11. http://dx.doi.org/10.1017/jie.2017.36

National Indigenous Australians Agency. (n.d.). *Indigenous student success program*. Australian Government. https://www.niaa.gov.au/indigenous-affairs/education/indigenous-student-success-program

National Indigenous Higher Education Advisory Council. (2006, March). *Improving Indigenous outcomes and enhancing Indigenous culture and knowledge in Australian higher education* [Report to the Minister for Education, Science and Training]. Department of Education, Science and Training. http://citeseerx.ist.psu.edu/viewdoc/download?doi=10.1.1.173.2525&rep=rep1&type=pdf

National Indigenous Higher Education Advisory Council. (2011). *National Indigenous higher education workforce strategy*. https://www.dese.gov.au/aboriginal-and-torres-strait-islander-higher-education/resources/national-indigenous-higher-education-workforce-strategy

Oliver, R., Grote, E., Rochecouste, J. & Dann, T. (2016). Indigenous student perspectives on support and impediments at university. *Australian Journal of Indigenous Education*, *45*(1), 23–35. https://doi.org/10.1017/jie.2015.16

Oliver, R., Rochecouste, J., Bennell, D., Anderson, R., Cooper, I., Forrest, S. & Exell, M. (2013a). Understanding Australian Aboriginal tertiary student needs. *International Journal of Higher Education*, *2*(4), 52–64. http://doi.org/10.5430/ijhe.v2n4p52

Oliver, R., Rochecouste, J. & Grote, E. (2013b). *The transition of Aboriginal and Torres Strait Islander students into higher education*. Office for Learning and Teaching. https://ltr.edu.au/resources/SI11_2137_Oliver_Report_2013.pdf

Page, S., DiGregorio, K. D. & Farrington, S. (1997, November 30–December 4). *The student experiences study: Understanding the factors that affect Aboriginal and Torres Strait Islander students' academic success* [Conference presentation]. Annual Conference of the Australian Association for Research in Education, Brisbane, Australia. https://www.aare.edu.au/data/publications/1997/digrk446.pdf

Pechenkina, E. & Anderson, I. (2011, September). *Consultation paper on Indigenous Australian higher education: Trends, initiatives and policy implications* (Commissioned Research Paper No. 1). Commonwealth of Australia. https://www.dese.gov.au/access-and-participation/resources/background-paper-indigenous-australian-higher-education-trends-initiatives-and-policy-implications

Rigney, L.-I. & Neill, B. (2018, June). *Higher education outcomes for Indigenous Australians: Barriers and enablers to participation and completion*. Centre for Research in Social Inclusion and Education. https://apo.org.au/sites/default/files/resource-files/2018-06/apo-nid201806.pdf

Schulz, P., Dunne, C. L., Burdett-Jones, D., Gamble, N. S., Kosiak, M. M., Neal, J. M. & Baker, G. E. (2018). Evaluation of strategies designed to enhance student engagement and success of Indigenous midwifery students in an away-from-base bachelor of midwifery program in Australia. A qualitative research study. *Nurse Education Today*, *63*, 59–63. https://doi.org/10.1016/j.nedt.2018.01.026

Schwartz, M. (2018). Retaining our best: Imposter syndrome, cultural safety, complex lives and Indigenous student experiences of law school. *Legal Education Review, 28*(2), 1–22. https://doi.org/10.53300/001c.7455

Taylor, E. V., Lalovic, A. & Thompson, S. C. (2019). Beyond enrolments: A systematic review exploring the factors affecting the retention of Aboriginal and Torres Strait Islander health students in the tertiary education system. *International Journal for Equity Health, 18*(1), Article 136. https://doi.org/10.1186/s12939-019-1038-7

Uink, B., Hill, B., Day, A. & Martin, G. (2019). 'Wings to fly': A case study of supporting Indigenous student success through a whole-of-university approach. *Australian Journal of Indigenous Education, 48*(2), 206. https://doi.org/10.1017/jie.2019.11

Universities Australia. (2017). *Indigenous strategy 2017–2020*. https://www.universitiesaustralia.edu.au/wp-content/uploads/2019/06/Indigenous-Strategy-v16-1.pdf

Universities Australia. (2019). *Indigenous strategy first annual report*. https://www.universitiesaustralia.edu.au/wp-content/uploads/2019/06/20190304-Final-Indigenous-Strategy-Report-v2-2.pdf

Universities Australia. (2020, January). *Indigenous strategy annual report*. https://www.universitiesaustralia.edu.au/wp-content/uploads/2020/02/Indigenous-strategy-second-annual-report.pdf

Universities Australia. (2011, October). *National best practice framework for Indigenous cultural competency in Australian universities*. https://www.universitiesaustralia.edu.au/wp-content/uploads/2019/06/National-Best-Practice-Framework-for-Indigenous-Cultural-Competency-in-Australian-Universities.pdf

Usher, K., Lindsay, D., Miller, M. & Miller, A. (2005). Challenges faced by Indigenous nursing students and strategies that aided their progress in the course: A descriptive study. *Contemporary Nurse, 19*(1–2), 17–31. https://doi.org/10.5172/conu.19.1-2.17

Zepke, N. & Leach, L. (2005). Integration and adaptation: Approaches to the student retention and achievement puzzle. *Active Learning in Higher Education, 6*(1), 46–59. https://doi.org/10.1177/1469787405049946

1 Key concepts and conditions for student success

This chapter introduces key concepts and influences related to higher education success. The topics are sequenced so that they move the reader from an initial focus on academic learning demands and expectations and what these mean for under-prepared learners, and then through concepts associated with students' own attributes and their position as Indigenous learners in the university, including critical factors related to Indigenous students' study conditions. The chapter then concludes with a brief summary of implications for the support staff effort.

Independent learning and independent learners

Unlike teachers in the school sector, university academics do not necessarily follow up with students to ensure that they are understanding or mastering academic content, that they can complete academic tasks, or that they are on track to submit assessments. Higher education expects students to be self-motivated and independent in how they conduct their learning and meet academic demands. Because of this distinct difference between learning at school and university, all commencing higher education students experience a transition period as they adjust to higher education learning demands and expectations. In numerous studies of Indigenous students' initial academic learning experiences, students have made statements similar to 'I didn't know what I was doing and how I was supposed to do it.'[1] Although there is increasing attention by universities and academics to first-year transition strategies for all higher education students,[2] the transition can be a much more daunting, complex, and lengthier process for Indigenous students. It is a mistake to assume that first-year transition pedagogies in degree programs and the standard university-wide student service provisions are sufficient for many Indigenous students to meet higher education expectations.

In the higher education literature, the concept of independent learning is ill-defined, open to multiple interpretations, and mostly discussed with regard to academic teaching design.[3] However, 'independent learners … can be described as proactive, self-motivated and resourceful (make use of available resources) individuals who are able to self-direct, monitor and self-regulate their learning progress towards achieving their learning goals.'[4] From the student support perspective, an independent learner has 'the capacity or ability to take charge of [their] learning' and is willing or motivated to do so.[5]

DOI: 10.4324/9781003326458-2

In becoming an independent learner, a student is involved in the process of *learning how to learn* in the higher education setting. This task is in addition to Indigenous students having to overcome gaps in the prior or assumed knowledge they require to understand and engage with new and unfamiliar academic content in their courses. This 'learning how to learn' process, or, as students have expressed it, working out what they are meant to do and how to do it, adds an additional layer of effort for students and increases the amount of time required for academic tasks.

Learning how to learn requires students to determine what they must do to manage and complete academic tasks successfully.[6] These tasks vary between subjects, disciplines, and throughout semester and year levels. They do not necessarily include just the required assessment tasks but also encompass various academic skills and strategies associated with different aspects of the learning process, for example, academic reading, research, note-taking, and planning skills. Students must determine what knowledge, skills, and strategies they need to apply to different tasks and at different stages of a long task, such as an assignment. This involves extending the repertoire of skills and strategies they learnt at school, in their community, or in the workplace. Just as importantly, knowing how to learn at university also involves understanding how to be organised and how to keep up with learning tasks. As part of this, students must also determine what to do when things do not go according to plan, when they become distracted, run out of time, lose motivation, or feel like giving up. Having strategies for these instances helps students to persist and develop resilience.[7]

Thus, the process of becoming an independent learner requires the development of a new set of capabilities, which involves acquiring new knowledge about how to learn and new skills and strategies for doing so. These capabilities will also enable students to keep learning and operating in changing knowledge environments in their future careers; therefore, it is important that they develop them effectively.

Although it is understood that higher education learning requires students to develop *higher-order cognitive* skills, students also require two other sets of skills to become successful independent learners: *metacognitive* and *affective* skills. Cognitive skills include the mental abilities associated with individual learning, such as processing information, logic and reasoning, problem-solving, memory/recall, attention or focus, and language skills. Higher-order cognitive skills include the ability to analyse, synthesise, and evaluate information, which, in higher education, involves critical thinking and analysis.[8] Metacognition is defined as 'the awareness of and knowledge about one's own thinking.'[9] In learning, it refers to a student's awareness of how they are functioning in their learning. Metacognitive awareness includes students' knowledge about themselves as learners and knowledge of strategies that will help them complete a task efficiently. Metacognitive skills (also referred to as strategies) refer to a student's ability to implement this knowledge skilfully and apply appropriate strategies to different tasks or stages of tasks.[10]

Metacognitive knowledge and skills help students self-direct their cognitive or mental processing of subject content towards a particular aim and regulate their motivation to work at the task until it is completed. Some students are so practised in these skills that they seem a 'natural' part of their learning. However, these are acquired skills, and many Indigenous students are not practised in them when they arrive at university. For developing metacognitive skills, students need to become aware of how they approach learning, be able to judge whether the way they approach learning is effective and produces results, and be able to determine when they need to adjust, adapt, or change their learning strategies and study behaviours to meet the specific demands of various academic tasks. This involves skills associated with planning, self-monitoring, and self-evaluating.

Affective skills are those related to managing moods, feelings, or attitudes, for example, how to recognise and manage unproductive negative emotions and reactions, which can interfere with a student's ability to engage in learning opportunities, maintain motivation, maintain productive relations with their peers, and persist with, keep on track, or complete tasks.[11] For example, in student interviews, it was revealed that some students were hesitant to ask questions and/or engage in classroom discussions due to feeling nervous, anxious, or embarrassed. One student reported not attending course tutorials for over a year for these reasons.[12] Another student reported she did not engage in Indigenous studies tutorials because she was scared of showing anger or frustration towards the opinions of non-Indigenous peers.[13] Learning how to manage these emotional responses to learning and social situations contributes to developing resilience when encountering setbacks.

Integrating these skill sets—cognitive, metacognitive, and affective—enables students to feel in control of their learning. To reiterate, from the support perspective, an independent learner is one who can exert control over their learning; as one student noted: 'You know there's no teachers chasing you up for work … and I found that you have to become independent very quick[ly]. You have to start to take control of all that learning.'[14]

Indigenous students without the necessary capabilities to exert control over their learning require support or assistance from others to develop the awareness, knowledge, and skills they need to be strategic and efficient in approaching learning and study. Academically underprepared students almost always require individual assistance to develop the higher-order cognitive processing skills they need and the metacognitive and affective capabilities they need to control and manage their learning. However, some academically well-prepared Indigenous students are likely to need some assistance to develop the metacognitive and affective capabilities to be more in control of their learning and more strategic in their efforts to do well. Higher education students have heavy demands on their time; they need to use strategic learning methods to be efficient learners.

It takes time to learn how to take charge or control of learning and become independent enough to require only minimal levels of support. However, regarding students' movements towards independence, it is important to note the following. The length of time it takes to become relatively independent varies between individuals, and, in all likelihood, it will not be a linear progression. Rather, for any individual, the ability to feel in control will vary between tasks and between subjects. It will also depend on a student's level of readiness for university, their particular strengths and weaknesses, their personalities and attributes, and the nature of the challenges that arise in their learning and personal lives. This implies that support staff must understand students' areas of challenge—both academic and personal.[15]

It is most important in the context of Indigenous student support that independent learning is not interpreted as students learning in isolation or on their own. Successful learners learn in an interactive process with their lecturers, tutors, peers, texts, and other services.[16] Independent learning in the support context should also not be equated with independent and self-directed projects that are sometimes set for students by academics. In the support context, the emphasis is always on assisting students to take charge of their own learning.

Student readiness for academic learning and university

In the higher education literature, student readiness for university has been defined 'as the level of preparation a student needs in order to enrol and succeed, without remediation in a credit-bearing program at a higher education institution.'[17] Many university students are not fully prepared for higher education study because they are yet to develop the various sets of knowledge, skills, or capabilities required to meet the expectations and methods of the disciplines and higher education learning.[18] Under-preparedness makes learning more challenging for most Indigenous students. Pre-entry activities and pathway, preparation, and enabling programs are the primary mechanisms for improving the readiness of prospective and enrolled Indigenous students. In the absence of these or in the event they do not prepare students sufficiently (which is often the case), students begin their undergraduate degrees unprepared for the demands, expectations, and challenges they will encounter. Three areas of readiness need to be considered in the Indigenous preparation/enabling and undergraduate student contexts: academic, psychosocial, and emotional readiness.

Academic readiness assumes students have sufficient prior academic content and academic skills to independently engage with new and unfamiliar content and develop the higher-order skills needed to achieve success in a chosen course.[19]

Psychosocial readiness has also been identified as important to success.[20] The term 'psychosocial' refers to the interrelations between social factors and an individual's psychological patterns of thinking, feeling, and behavioural responses.[21] Social factors include students' relationships with others in the university social and learning environments. As a factor in higher education readiness, psychosocial readiness intersects with academic readiness and refers to the relation between students' individual attributes and their engagement with learning processes, demands, and other expectations in the university environment. These attributes include a range of 'self' concepts, such as self-confidence, self-efficacy, and the ability to self-regulate.[22] These 'self' concepts are in addition to individual student attributes or behaviours, such as motivation, commitment, persistence, and resilience, which also influence a student's approach to academic learning and study efforts.[23] Those who work in Indigenous student support know from experience that these latter attributes are instrumental to the success of many academically underprepared Indigenous students. Thousands of Indigenous students without prior academic requisites for success have succeeded through the strength of their personal attributes, often recognised by support staff in terms such as 'grit,' 'determination,' 'motivation,' and 'commitment.'[24]

Alongside psychosocial readiness, it is common for Indigenous students to be ill-prepared for the *emotional aspects of academic learning* in the teaching, peer, and social environments of the university. Anxieties and frustrations associated with the following can all affect a student's motivation and ability to engage or persist with learning and higher education study: the challenges of academic learning and performance; the sensitivities concerning alternative entry conditions; the sensitivities regarding the treatment of Indigenous content in courses (or its absence); everyday experiences of racism and real or perceived discrimination by peers, lecturers, and university services; feelings of isolation, discomfort, and not belonging in the academic and social environments of the university; and challenges arising from students' personal circumstances, such as the loss of usual social support networks, loneliness, homesickness, and other personal worries and pressures. At least one of these (and often more) were mentioned by almost all students we interviewed, and they are well documented in the Indigenous higher education student experience literature.[25]

Being underprepared in these three areas of readiness—academic, psychosocial, and emotional—can affect Indigenous students' confidence levels, belief in their ability to succeed, ability to engage in classroom discussions, and motivation to persist with their study. As those who work in Indigenous student support know from experience, being underprepared can also produce a range of negative emotions that affect the students' chances of academic success and their health and socio-emotional wellbeing, for example, feeling overwhelmed, anxiety, panic, frustration, anger, stress, distress, depressed moods, and, in extreme cases, trauma.

Even when this is not the case, being underprepared means that the student's workload is increased. Underprepared students have to add to the normal student load the extra time it takes to do academic tasks, such as the additional time for reading and understanding course content and drafting essays. That is, more time must be spent developing and mastering skills alongside mastering the course content, but mastering content is made more difficult and takes more time with lower skill levels.

The primary role of student support staff is to assist underprepared students to develop the capabilities (knowledge, skills, and strategies) required to perform their academic tasks. Students' capabilities in these areas can be developed if they are given appropriate support and strategies to help them manage. However, students' support needs vary according to their levels or areas of under-preparation, their individual attributes, the challenges associated with specific disciplines and subjects, and any challenges in other areas of their lives that affect their ability to overcome the academic challenges they encounter.

Without knowing individual students' levels or areas of readiness and under-preparation, it is difficult to understand a student's needs and, therefore, what level of support they might require. Unless all students' levels of preparedness can be determined early on, academic course advice and selection-for-entry decisions risk setting students up to fail. Further, unless students' academic progress and personal challenges are monitored throughout their studies, support strategies for students risk not meeting individual students' needs for tailored forms of assistance or not being applied in time to prevent failures.

While supplementary tutors can do some academic capacity developmental work, it needs to be considered that there is a complex interplay between the academic, psychosocial, and socio-emotional factors that affect student learning and achievement levels.[26] It cannot be assumed that all supplementary tutors assist students in all three areas or have the knowledge and skills to do so.[27] This implies that academic and pastoral support staff will need to share information and work closely together to meet a student's multiple or intersecting needs and that academic support advisers will also require some knowledge of what aspects of learning a tutor and student should focus on and how well the relationship between the tutor and student is working.

Sometimes, academically able, relatively independent, or high achieving Indigenous students will flounder, underperform, or fail. *Academic underperformance* is different from *academic under-preparation*; however, the outcomes are often similar. The reasons for students' underperformance should always be investigated so that appropriate interventions or strategies can be provided to meet student needs.

Student agency

The three sections that follow—agency, self-efficacy, and self-regulation—should be read in sequence. Together, they highlight the capabilities (knowledge, skills, and strategies) students need to take control of their learning and become independent and successful learners. These concepts are associated with students' beliefs in their ability to influence their outcomes, and their purposefulness and strategic skilfulness in learning: 'to be an agent is to influence intentionally one's functioning and life circumstances … [People] are contributors to their life circumstances, not just products of them.'[28] This view of human agency stems from social cognitive theory, presenting a theory of human motivation, adaptation, and change that aims to disrupt the oppositional dualities of individual agency versus social structure, individualism versus collectivism, and personal autonomy versus interdependence, on which many theories of cultural psychology theory pivot.[29]

Agentive theory is premised on the idea that individuals' abilities to exert control over their futures are determined by the interplay between environmental, intra-personal, and behavioural factors. It emphasises the role of an individual's ability to influence their own actions, behaviours, and outcomes within the constraints of these three sets of determinants. To exert influence, an individual must form an intention and a future-directed goal relevant to that intention and plan to act on their intention. They must also believe that they can achieve the anticipated outcome of their proposed actions, as well as visualise and anticipate the future outcome of their actions, in order to motivate themselves to put their plan into action. They then need to be able to regulate their behaviour to guide their planned actions towards the intended outcome. Finally, they must then reflect on their own functioning through this process to make adjustments to achieve future goals, if necessary.[30] According to Bandura, '[t]hrough cognitive self-guidance, humans can visualise futures that act on the present; construct, evaluate, and modify alternative courses of action to gain valued outcomes, and override environmental influences.'[31]

The concept of human agency is much debated and, for our purposes in this book, we note but do not engage the larger and theoretically complex literature on human agency. For example, the literature transverses psychology, sociology, education, political theory, and philosophy and is applied to discussions and contexts beyond education. The ideas used in this book are embedded in educational psychology and reflect a sociological perspective.

In the higher education context, it is important to recognise the constraints that environmental, intra-personal, and behavioural determinants impose on Indigenous students and avoid holding students responsible for the factors they cannot control. However, the concept of agency is worth introducing here for several reasons. First, there is a relationship between personal agency and students' efforts to learn and to persist. Second, in the higher education literature, student persistence is primarily discussed regarding its implications for institutional efforts to retain students. Institutional efforts include services and strategies to enable or encourage students to persist when encountering challenges. However, students must still make an *active and purposeful effort* to benefit from those institutional aids. Thus, in Indigenous student support, we need to be concerned with how to develop and support students to be active and purposeful in their efforts. Third, the concept of agency resonates in the Indigenous sector because it expresses the Indigenous community's desire and capacity to *control decisions* that affect Indigenous interests and futures. Agency serves both individual and collective autonomy.

Individual agency is largely assumed in terms of student efforts and higher education pedagogy and teaching traditions. The agency theory positions students as the agents of their own learning. Indigenous students need to exert some control over their own actions, choices, and decisions to be agents of their own learning.

Simply recognising the agency of individual students does not mean students have the necessary attributes and capabilities required to act in an agentive way and mediate the effects of environmental or social influences through their own actions. The role of student support is to assist students to develop the individually indicated knowledge, skills, resources, and strategies that will enable them to exert influence and eventual control over their functioning as students. Thus, two key activators of student agency—self-efficacy and self-regulation—need some explanation.

Self-efficacy and academic self-efficacy

While there is a relationship between personal agency and an individual's ability to persevere or persist when they encounter negative influences, 'unless people believe they can produce desired effects by their actions, they have little incentive to act, or to persevere in the face of difficulties'.[32] This self-belief in one's capacity to achieve a desired outcome is conceptualised as *self-efficacy* in social cognitive theory. According to social cognitive theory, self-efficacy beliefs are central to activating individual agency, how individuals use goals as personal challenges, how much effort they make to achieve a goal, their motivation to persist when they encounter a difficulty, and their resilience when encountering a setback.[33] Further:

> self-efficacy beliefs … affect whether individuals think in self-enhancing or self-debilitating ways, how well they motivate themselves and persevere in the face of difficulties, the quality of their emotional well-being and their vulnerability to stress and depression, and the choices they make at important decisional points.[34]

A student's self-belief in their capacity to achieve academically at the expected levels is conceptualised as *academic self-efficacy*. A student must believe they can succeed in an academic task or achieve the goals they set for themselves. If they do not, they can quickly lose the motivation to persist when they encounter an obstacle. Therefore, high levels of academic self-efficacy can be considered 'a vital personal resource' for students' motivation, persistence, and achievement.[35] Academic self-efficacy is related to achievement outcomes, students' choices and decision-making, persistence with difficult tasks, learning engagement, and the use of strategic study skills.[36]

Whether an individual has high or low self-efficacy beliefs is influenced by their perception of their ability or competence to achieve a desired outcome. This means that a student with high self-efficacy believes that they have enough competency to influence their outcomes. A student with a strong self-belief 'in their capabilities is more likely to approach difficult tasks as challenges to be mastered rather than as threats to be avoided.'[37]

An individual with low self-efficacy often has negative thought patterns that work against purposeful actions and confirm their beliefs that they cannot exert control over their situation, circumstances, or outcomes. In some cases, a student's academic efficacy beliefs may be influenced by a general belief that their intelligence or abilities cause their achievement outcomes. When encountering learning challenges, such a student may believe that a learning task is difficult because they are not smart enough or that students who do better than them are smarter than they are. However, self-efficacy does not refer to an individual's self-belief about their general ability or intelligence and should not be confused with more general 'self' concepts, such as self-concept, self-esteem, or self-worth.[38] Rather, academic self-efficacy is related to a student's belief about their capacity to meet the challenges of a specific academic task at hand. For example, a student may have high self-efficacy for oral presentations and low self-efficacy for written essays or high self-efficacy for essay writing and low self-efficacy for exams.[39] This is likely to affect how such a student approaches these different tasks, including their emotional states (e.g., levels of anxiety, stress, or enthusiasm) and motivational states (e.g., purposeful action or avoidance), and thus, the degree of effort they make. Therefore, self-efficacy beliefs relate to how an individual judges their current level of competence regarding the challenges of a task.

It is also important to consider that a student's experiences of success or failure in specific tasks provide the basis for their beliefs about their competency for future similar tasks.[40] For example, a student who receives a mark close to a pass on an assignment may be more likely to believe they can improve on their past effort and pass the next assignment than a student who receives a very low mark. A student who has improved their essay writing skills incrementally may be more likely to believe they can eventually improve from a pass to a credit to a distinction grade. As one student stated: 'I just don't want to pass, but I want to see myself progressing, and that might be in each task.'[41] A student who experiences success in a challenging task they have persisted with is more likely to lift their self-efficacy beliefs and, as a result, be motivated to make an effort to persist with future challenges rather than avoid them, reduce their effort, or give up.

Thus, a student's academic self-efficacy beliefs can be developed to enhance persistence and increase their levels of mastery when encountering difficult challenges if they have experiences of success, even if these successes are incremental or produce only small improvements. This has implications for the timing and effectiveness of support interventions. It implies these interventions must be timed to assist with challenges or prevent failures, including failures in subjects and difficulties or failures in smaller tasks and assessments. Numerous students we interviewed reported that as they worked out what to do and how to do it, they felt more competent and began to believe they would complete their studies if they concentrated on incrementally improving on their previous marks. This indicates a shift towards being more focused on task-oriented goals and outcomes as the path to achieving career or other personal goals and long-term outcomes.

There are four primary sources of self-efficacy[42] that can be related to academic self-efficacy. It is useful for support staff to be familiar with these because these are also methods for increasing academic self-efficacy beliefs:

1   *Success in mastering specific tasks* is the most effective source—the more a student experiences success in a task, the more likely they are to believe they can succeed in a future task.

2   *Vicariously experiencing or observing other's success*, such as those who are considered similar to, rather than too different from, the individual, is a source of self-efficacy. This suggests that Indigenous students' observations of other successful Indigenous students, academics, or professionals are more likely to positively influence their self-belief in their capacity than their observations of non-Indigenous students or academics. Indigenous role models are more likely to be perceived as having overcome similar challenges. Other successful underprepared students might also act as a source.

3   *Verbally persuading students* that they can master an activity often leads to greater efforts by the student.

4   *Altering a student's interpretation of their emotional states* is a source of self-efficacy. For example, students who focus on their weaknesses rather than their strengths can be assisted to reflect on how these negative thoughts demotivate them and undermine their efforts. Students who feel stressed, who panic or freeze, or who feel they are not capable can be helped to recognise the distorting role that anxiety and negativity have in their self-judgement about their level of competence and how this prevents them from engaging fully in the learning tasks designed to develop their competencies.

Regarding these four sources of self-efficacy, we suggest that using role models and verbal persuasion (sources 2 and 3) are commonly practised in the Indigenous student support sector, and there is strong anecdotal evidence that these are effective and sufficient for some students. For example, a student stated that they were inspired by the Indigenous people working in the IEU and that it was 'very encouraging to me. I like seeing people there in those positions, and I feel "right, *I* can do that" … I've got a bit more belief in myself that I can succeed in university.'[43]

However, we also suggest that Indigenous support staff have less control over the first and last sources outlined above (sources 1 and 4), at least for the Indigenous students who may require assistance or benefit from these methods. Sources 1 and 4 are student success in mastering specific tasks and how students perceive and interpret their emotional states. As most Indigenous student support staff know from experience, these are very much implicated in students' ability to manage challenges, control their learning, and maintain socio-emotional wellbeing.

Studies have also revealed that these methods for increasing academic self-efficacy work best when learning activities or assistance are structured to enable success and avoid failures.[44] Without this element, methods or strategies for improving academic self-efficacy may not influence students positively but reinforce negative beliefs instead. For example, simply telling a student that they can succeed if they make more effort, without assessing whether they have the necessary skills and strategies to complete a task successfully, is unlikely to be effective and may also discourage them from seeking help in the future. The role that structured activities play in students' efficacy beliefs is recognised in academic teaching and learning practices that adhere to the first-year transition pedagogy principles. The transition pedagogy or teaching method encourages academics to scaffold academic skills development into early assessments for commencing students, so they learn how to conduct a task in a structured way with feedback given at each stage to improve their chances of a final successful outcome.[45] Support staff can contribute to this learning process by keeping abreast of students' assessment tasks and providing support and feedback regarding their efforts. Supplementary tutors are very helpful for students in this process, as many students reported in interviews.[46]

The emphasis on the relationship between structured assistance and achieving success also has significant implications for the student support effort for following up with students who have been assisted with a specific challenge. For example, it may not be enough to verbally advise a student to plan their approach to a learning task and then leave them to it. A student might not know what such a plan should include, be able to judge how much time an aspect of a task will need, or have the skills and capabilities to execute their plan successfully. This implies that support staff must assess students' competency levels concerning any task for which they require assistance. This can be informally assessed through the questioning techniques support staff use, for example, by asking students to show what they have thought about or attempted so far. It also implies that staff need to work with students on ways to construct a plan for the particular purpose required and/or provide good examples, ask them to bring back their attempts for further feedback, and after students have implemented their plan, follow up on how their plans worked and what the learning outcome was to determine whether the student will need further assistance in this area.

This provides a structure for support efforts regarding any student need and was brought to our attention by academic support staff in our previous university. Their practice of always asking a student what they had done so far to address an academic challenge had two benefits. First, it enabled staff to determine what the student could do and where they were stuck. Second, questioning and feedback from the staff modelled a process for students to reflect on how they were conducting a task. Similarly, in our study, we found that asking the follow-up question, 'what did you do when faced with this challenge?', prompted some students to reflect more on what they did and how they were conducting their learning. In subsequent interviews, several students noted that the previous interview had got them thinking more about their approaches to learning and what they could change. This strategy is also useful when assisting students with personal or administrative issues. For example, a pastoral support staff member at our previous university often accompanied overwhelmed or anxious students to other university services and waited outside to check on how they were feeling in the aftermath. This was often enough to help a student to manage independently in subsequent similar situations.

It is also important that staff check that students' academic self-efficacy beliefs are relatively accurate or consistent with their actual competencies.[47] For example, a student with an over-inflated self-efficacy belief relative to their competence level may make excuses or blame others for their difficulties or low outcomes rather than reflect on their own competence levels or need for assistance. An over-inflated self-efficacy belief may be a mask for underlying anxiety or fear of failure.

In summary, academic self-efficacy beliefs influence students' approaches to challenging tasks, the efforts they apply to a task, and their motivation to persist with a task and, thus, affect their chances of achieving a successful outcome. In turn, success in a task provides the basis for students' ongoing beliefs in their capabilities when undertaking other challenging tasks, which assists their motivation, degree of effort, the likelihood of attempting more challenging tasks in the future, and the extent to which they can control their learning. Student support should be aware of the role that incremental successes play in students' motivations to persist when they encounter challenges and the role that students' competency levels for a task have in developing higher self-efficacy beliefs. Staff also need to keep in mind that self-efficacy beliefs activate individual agency and influence the sense of purposefulness and confidence with which students go about learning and study tasks. Assisting students to develop the skills and strategies they need to activate agency and self-efficacy beliefs is a core part of the academic support officer's role.

In any attempt to judge a student's self-efficacy beliefs, it is most important to draw judgements from the context of a specific task or domain (e.g., essay writing) and not from something general. Further, there is no benefit from using the term 'self-efficacy' with students. The concept is presented in this book to alert staff to the role of a student's mindset in their approach to learning tasks and emphasise the links between a student's belief that they can influence their outcomes through their own efforts and their competency level and experiences of success.

While discussing their growing confidence in their ability to succeed, one student remarked, 'what has changed is what I believe about my ability and my self-belief.'[48] A former enabling student explained the importance of their own thinking when encountering learning challenges:

> My attitude has changed a lot from coming in till now … I don't look at something and be like, 'this is going to be so hard, and I can't do it.' Like, it's learning, so no matter what, it's not going to be easy. So, my whole mindset's changed.[49]

Another student discussed how they had developed to become more active in their learning and the role of feelings of competency in their growing confidence:

> I started out in university real timid, didn't know what was going on … Now, everything's starting to make more sense, I'm developing my academic skills and becoming more confident, and my learning is starting to become more and more purposeful.[50]

Self-regulation

When applied to learning, agentive theory positions students as 'anticipative, purposive, and self-evaluating proactive regulators of their motivation and actions.'[51] The ability to self-regulate learning is strongly related to achieving outcomes and is an indicator of success and control over the learning process.

Self-regulated learning is 'an active, constructive process whereby learners set goals for their learning and then attempt to monitor, regulate and control their cognition, motivation and behaviours, guided and constrained by their goals and the contextual features in the environment.'[52] In simpler terms, the process of self-regulation provides the link between students' learning goals and their actions to reach them—that is, self-regulation is 'the self-directive process by which learners transform their mental abilities into academic skills.'[53]

The concept of self-regulated learning is central to Indigenous student success in higher education for several reasons. First, the ability of students to be self-regulated learners is an expectation and an implicit condition of higher education learning.[54] Second, self-regulated learning is a foundation for independent and lifelong learning.[55] Third, student skills and behaviours associated with self-regulation of learning are considered predictors of student success.[56] Self-regulated learners have the knowledge, skills, and strategies to control their learning, and Indigenous graduates will require the abilities and attributes of independent and lifelong learners throughout their professional lives.

Students' abilities to self-regulate learning have been used to explain some of the individual differences in achievement among students, irrespective of whether these students happen to be advantaged or disadvantaged in education.[57] A student's ability to self-regulate their learning may help explain, for example, why one Indigenous school leaver with a high tertiary ranking, no financial worries and a place in a residential college on campus flounders at university while an academically underprepared mature-aged, single parent manages to progress very well on few resources and in the face of onerous demands on their time. One academically able student, reflecting on his underperformance during his early years, noted his lack of awareness about how he approached learning and how it affected his ability to meet workload demands: 'Because I didn't struggle [to learn], I didn't have any self-discipline when it came to study. I'm really bad at forcing myself to learn stuff because it's always been easy, and I never got the skills to do that.'[58]

The literature regarding self-regulation is theoretically dense and detailed for the novice. There is a range of theoretical orientations and, therefore, no singular definition. Self-regulated learning is conceptualised via various theoretical models and overlapping constructs and is discussed across a broad range of empirical studies, including in schooling and higher education. Although there is a range of models for self-regulated learning, we do not think it particularly useful to explain them here.[59] Instead, we engage some of the literature that outlines the processes and components of self-regulation so that support staff can gain a little more understanding about what is involved in a student's ability to self-regulate learning and to draw some implications for the student support effort.

The many descriptions of self-regulated learning processes in the research literature stress the interplay between students' cognitive, metacognitive, motivational, and affective processes and how these interact to influence a student's achievement of specific goals. (Cognitive skills refer to mental processing skills; metacognitive skills aid directive and strategic processes or strategies; motivational processes refer to a student's will or willingness to apply themselves to a task; affective processes refer to the feelings experienced while conducting a task.)[60] Other descriptions stress that how well a student manages the interplay between these processes as they conduct a learning task also influences their forward management and control over future learning task goals in a cyclical developmental process.[61]

There are three main phases of self-regulation that theorists draw attention to: (1) forethought (what a student does to prepare for a learning task); (2) performance (what a student does during a task); and (3) reflection (what a student does after the task). Sometimes these three phases are referred to as pre-action, action, and post-action phases. Self-regulated students attend to subtasks in each of these phases.[62]

For example, in the *forethought or pre-action phase*, the self-regulated learner thinks about such things as what a task will involve or require them to do, what they want to achieve (their goal for this specific task), whether the task needs to be divided into parts and stages, what aspects of the task might present challenges and whether they should seek guidance or have a strategy for managing any anticipated difficulty, how much time the task might take, and what other demands, academic or otherwise, will conflict with or distract them from completing the task on time. Having assessed these, the self-regulated learner will consider their strategies and the resources required to undertake the task and then plan a sequence of actions and a schedule to help them complete the task.

In the *performance or action phase*, the self-regulated learner carries out the task by executing their plans and applying their strategies while also monitoring whether what they are doing is helping them move towards their goal or complete the task on time (metacognitive monitoring). They adapt their strategies as they go, if necessary. As part of this self-monitoring process, the student also monitors and manages their emotions and behaviours in a continuous effort to maintain their motivation in a positive, productive, and efficient way. This is likely to include managing the common tendencies to procrastinate, stress, lose optimism, or become unproductively anxious or distracted. In this stage, a self-regulated learner will typically seek assistance if they become stuck, overwhelmed, or unable to keep on track or keep going. If they are already strategically skilful, they might adjust their original plan or use a strategy they have found from a previous similar situation. Many students we interviewed discussed their strategies for managing their study behaviours and the ups and downs that occur while executing their study plans. However, this was not the case for all students.

In the *reflection or post-action phase*, the self-regulated learner reflects on their efforts concerning their achievement outcomes, including the effectiveness of their planning, their learning strategies, their emotional responses, how they managed distractions, and how they stayed motivated. These self-reflections include the integration of formal and informal feedback from others. Reflection and the integration of feedback enables the self-regulated learner to appraise their efforts and whether they would apply the same level of effort and strategies again, make adjustments, or try alternatives for similar tasks in the future.

A self-regulated learner will roughly follow the patterns described above. However, the process can be much messier for most students, as we all know from our own experiences. Learning to self-regulate is a learning experience itself and students need time to build a flexible repertoire of skills for managing different tasks and situations. Thus, it is important to understand that the way a student conducts a task is highly individual and can vary between tasks, subjects, and disciplines, and over time, as they progress through their course. It is also important to understand that how individual students conduct the same task varies between students. Individual students who self-regulate their learning determine what works for them for different sorts of tasks in a constant process of planning, monitoring, reflection, appraisal, and adjustment. Differences in approaches that emerge between students doing the same task or the same student doing different tasks reflect the idiosyncratic nature of learning, the different demands of academic tasks or disciplines, and the different influences on students.

It is very easy to assume that self-regulation only applies to assessment tasks or demands. However, these phases can be applied to any task relevant to the academic learning process, such as academic reading in preparation for tutorials, managing the reading load, managing time schedules, overcoming anxiety about participating in tutorial discussions, mastering university learning management systems, or evaluating information sources. Self-regulating students who approach these sorts of tasks, consciously or unconsciously, start with some sort of plan (a mental plan can suffice for some tasks), go about executing their plan, and reflect on whether what they are doing is working or worked and whether they will do it differently next time.

The ability to be a self-regulated learner applies to academic tasks and other contextual elements that affect a student's ability to keep up with, participate in, or fully engage with learning tasks successfully. These might include managing other demands on their time, emotions, interactions with academics, tutors, and peers, external pressures, avoidance behaviour, and distractions. Thus, self-regulation involves integrating cognitive, metacognitive, motivational, and affective skills and the motivation to apply them for purposeful and strategic purposes. Almost all the students we interviewed mentioned one or more of these contextual elements as examples of the challenges they confronted. These were as significant to their belief in their ability to succeed as their perceptions of their academic competency. This suggests that many more students could benefit from assistance to develop strategies and skills for managing these aspects of the learning process. This underlines the critical importance of pastoral support and the close relationship between pastoral and academic support practices for assisting students to feel in control of the many factors that can influence their outcomes.

Some students will self-regulate somewhat unconsciously while completing a task. Others will develop the skills and behaviours of self-regulation without much assistance from support staff. For example, a student who says that they started an assignment far too late to give it the time required to receive satisfactory marks and that in the future they will start assignments much earlier is self-appraising their performance and considering what they may need to do differently next time.

However, it cannot be assumed that all Indigenous students can self-regulate or have the knowledge and skills required to do so. For example, some may not think they need to think about planning their approach to a task, some may not have the knowledge and skills to plan well during the pre-action phase, and others may not be able to stay focused while they execute their plans or think about monitoring their performance as they progress. Many are unlikely to be accustomed to reflecting on whether they approached a task effectively or what they might change next time.

In light of this, some authors have highlighted the lesser focus that theory and research place on the components of student competencies for self-regulation.[63] These include the strategic knowledge, skills, and behaviours required to execute effective actions within each process phase. These might include, for example, the knowledge, skills, or behaviours needed to execute task analysis (e.g., what am I being asked to do?), task preparation and planning, seeking help, managing negative emotions, monitoring progress in a task, managing time, study behaviours and environments, managing levels of motivation and interest, interpreting feedback on their efforts, or making self-judgements and self-assessments. Support staff can provide assistance and guidance to students at this level.

For example, regarding monitoring and managing emotions, a student may be aware that exam stress leads them to collapse or freeze but not have thought about what contributes to their stress or have developed any effective strategies for reducing it. Another student might have stress-management techniques in the immediate sense, such as deep breathing or positive self-messaging, but not link exam stress to how they manage study notes and revision during the semester. Therefore, such a student may not develop a longer-term strategy for avoiding the panic associated with exam period stress, without some guidance. Further, a student who procrastinates or avoids tasks may not consider why or what strategies would help. Supporting students to talk about their responses to challenges is one way of encouraging them to reflect more thoughtfully on what they are doing and what they could do differently. Talking to students provides opportunities for staff to understand their situation more fully and provide advice or strategies.

It is important before or while giving students advice about managing learning challenges to listen carefully and assess whether they have the self-awareness, knowledge, and skills to recognise and manage some of these challenges more effectively. To do this, support staff should develop questioning techniques. For example, different students will have different underlying reasons for task avoidance, not simply a lack of self-discipline or interest. A student may have personal problems, problems with an academic, not understand the task, or not believe they have the competency to complete the task. They may be scared of failure, unable to find resources, or unable to ask for help. Thus, a large part of the support role involves determining how students are stuck and what sorts of skills, strategies, resources, and mindsets they need. Asking students what they think is the cause of their avoidance will prompt them to talk and think about what they have been doing or not doing and give staff a clearer idea about how best to advise and assist them.

Students also vary in their ability to reflect, self-appraise, and evaluate their approach to a task. Students easily overlook the reflection phase because they have often started other tasks by the time they receive formal feedback on assessment tasks. However, reflection and appraisal are integral to all descriptions of self-regulated learning and inform the cyclical process involved in developing the ability to self-regulate. Reflection on and appraisal of the effectiveness of their efforts includes integrating feedback from a range of formal and informal sources. This part of the process assists and motivates learners to vary and adjust their learning strategies and behaviours according to contextual demands and make intentional decisions about what they need to change in how they conduct their learning in future situations. Reflection and appraisal involve students appraising what they could change and noting what strategies and behaviours work for them and enable success. In our experience, a significant proportion of students do not have a practice of reflecting or do not know what to focus on or act on in their reflections. Such students can benefit from support staff conducting post-result meetings to give them some practice at this, particularly if there has been a failure or a drop in students' results.

In addition to sufficient levels of awareness, knowledge, and skills, the ability to self-regulate learning involves students having the will or motivation to *apply* these *strategically* to how they conduct their learning.[64] Strategic skilfulness is understood to develop through the student's practice of adjusting strategies and/or acquiring new strategies to meet similar or unfamiliar learning demands in the future. Success along the way develops a student's self-knowledge about how they learn and their strengths and weaknesses and helps them gain a positive and more confident perspective of their growing capabilities. Success and growing self-knowledge reinforce the will or motivation to persist through future challenges and the self-satisfaction that comes from improving their control over learning activities. The cyclical process of adjusting the way students learn builds their confidence in their ability to act and manage tasks independently when engaging in new and unfamiliar learning tasks and is critical to the development of independent or autonomous learners. Experienced and effective support staff will have observed this progression among the students they assist.

Although the ability to self-regulate is a learner-controlled process, developing this ability often requires students to seek assistance. This highlights that self-regulation processes, strategies, and skills can be learnt from others:

> Self-regulated students seek out help from others to improve their learning. What defines them as 'self-regulated' is not their reliance on socially isolated methods of learning, but rather their personal initiative, perseverance, and adoptive skill. Self-regulated students focus on how they activate, alter, and sustain specific learning practices in social as well as solitary contexts.[65]

This would seem to indicate that the development of students' help-seeking behaviours is an important component of assisting students to develop the self-regulatory skills and behaviours required to become more independent. It cannot be assumed that all students will seek assistance even if they can determine that they need help. Further, academic learning assistance is likely to fall short of student needs if it is conceptualised narrowly as remedial assistance with academic content and technical skills but overlooks assistance with the metacognitive, emotional, and behavioural competencies required for self-regulated learning.

As an example of how to normalise help-seeking behaviours, the academic support staff in our previous university undertook 'learning interviews' with all commencing students during the orientation period or soon after. This gave the staff important information regarding how the students were feeling about university study and provided opportunities for encouraging students to use all the supports available to them. However, it also prompted students to think about and reflect on the steps they were taking to be organised and to be realistic about the effort required to succeed. This simple and gentle practice began the process of developing commencing students' awareness of themselves as higher education learners.

The more a student develops the ability to self-regulate their learning, the more they develop and internalise the self-belief that they can intentionally influence their future outcomes through their choices, decisions, and actions. The more they develop self-belief in their own ability to achieve goals or improve incrementally, the more they are motivated to persist when they encounter challenges and pursue courses of action that they believe will help them achieve their goals. This might include proactive and well-considered actions to reduce academic loads or defer studies temporarily to establish the conditions required for achieving their goals. Such decisions are qualitatively different from decisions to 'give up' or 'walk away' that are associated with feelings of defeat or anger about university expectations and practices.

In summary, concepts of student agency, self-efficacy, and self-regulation illuminate the role that students' own efforts have in exerting some degree of control over their learning, success, and future outcomes. When encountering any challenging academic demands, a self-regulated learner can assess what they are required to do and make a plan for how to conduct the task, while being mindful of the personal and environmental challenges that might derail their efforts. They have developed strategies and skills to execute or adjust their plan or seek help if their plans go awry. They ask for help if they need it. They can reflect on and appraise the effectiveness of what they did to achieve their goals and make some strategic determinations about what they might change when undertaking a future task.

The ability to self-regulate learning should not be confused with a student's cognitive ability or level of academic performance. It concerns how they self-direct their learning process, which includes managing cognitive, motivational, metacognitive, and emotional dispositions and states prior to, during, and after attempts to meet a specific goal or task.[66] One highly self-regulated learner may achieve high grades while another might achieve much lower grades; however, both will demonstrate the ability to be in control of their learning and how they conduct it. It is also important to remember that although self-regulated learning is a hallmark of independent learning, self-regulated and independent learners continue to seek assistance when necessary. Further, from the support perspective, once a student is considered relatively independent in their learning, it does not follow that they will not need monitoring or assistance in the future.

Because agency, self-efficacy, and the processes and competencies involved in self-regulated learning are conceptualised as capabilities and because they are associated with persistence and independent and lifelong learning, we argue there is a need to focus on how to consciously or proactively support the development of all Indigenous students' capabilities in these aspects of the learning process.

The following quotes demonstrate that the students we interviewed recognised the value of developing their strategic skilfulness and managing their emotions:

> I know my main strengths and weaknesses now with studying, more so than I did in that first year and even in the first semester last year—I've learnt a lot more. I think it shows in my marks as well that I'm definitely a lot more efficient, and I try not to be so harsh on myself or stress myself as much.[67]

> I think that I probably wouldn't be here if I hadn't developed some knowledge of self about how I approach situations and how I react in certain situations.[68]

> The longer you've been at uni, the smarter you get with working. So that's what I've kind of like learnt is that it's not so much about working hard, I mean you've still got to work hard, but more so knowing where to put your time in working smart.[69]

Persistence

The concept of persistence represents a student's efforts 'to continue with studies despite negative influences acting upon them.'[70] Persisting in the face of inevitable challenges or setbacks is something that Indigenous students have to do (or learn to do) to continue studying and overcoming challenges that threaten their chances of success. While persistence is an effort that only students can make, many factors influence students' decisions to persist with or leave their studies. The next section, 'Motivation and persistence,' discusses the concepts related to students' abilities and motivations to persist with studying.

Student persistence is a primary interest of universities because it is implicated in the retention of students. The concept of retention is associated with 'the policies, actions and strategies of the institution to keep a student.'[71] Universities invest in students and have intellectual, reputational, and financial interests in retaining them until they complete their studies.

The logic of much research into persistence is that if the factors that influence students' decisions to persist or depart from their study can be determined and/or if the characteristics of persistent students can be identified or understood, then institutions can respond by developing policies, resources, services, or strategies that help students overcome obstacles and persist through to completion. Common institutional responses include enabling pathways, transition pedagogies and support for first-year students, teaching and learning centres and academic skills units, academic course advice and other student counselling services, student administration services, scholarships and other forms of financial support, and recreational and social activities to assist students' sense of belonging. Indigenous student support provisions are a specialised strand of the institutional response to help Indigenous student retention rates.

There is extensive international (including Australian) higher education literature relating to student persistence and departure from study and the retention and attrition of students.[72] The literature has been evolving over the last five decades, and Australian academics have actively contributed. This book does not represent this literature in any comprehensive or in-depth way. Suffice to say, thousands of studies worldwide have investigated and tested the validity of different factors and indicators associated with student persistence/institutional retention for different cohorts of students in varying educational contexts.

Broad analyses of investigations into the influences on persistence reveal the possible relevance of the following for students' persistence levels:

- students' prior academic performance; students' academic performance in their course of study (level of success or failure)
- students' social integration into the university or discipline (sense of belonging)
- students' personal attributes (e.g., self-confidence and optimistic/pessimistic traits)
- students' knowledge, attitudes and beliefs; students' commitment (e.g., to goals, study, workload, discipline, or university)
- students' background demographics, socio-economic status, prior experiences, and informal academic experiences
- students' finance issues
- students' external employment/work issues
- the extent and quality of student engagement (student learning/study and social behaviours in teaching/learning and institutional environments)

- students' satisfaction (captured in self-reporting surveys regarding various factors associated with courses, university support and services, quality of relationships/interactions with academics and peers, students' learning outcomes and progress)
- students' individual psychosocial and study skills (e.g., motivation to achieve, goal orientation, academic-related skills, and academic self-efficacy)
- university and student environments and institutions' culture (e.g., how a university responds to diversity, race/ethnicity, mature-age students, gender issues, or disability).[73]

Although not all studies test the relationships between these factors and student performance outcomes, correlations between persistence and student performance outcomes have been well established in the research literature.

There are two different aspects of persistence to consider from the Indigenous student support perspective that align with support staff responsibilities and for which students require support. One is the support that assists students to persist with academic learning tasks so that they experience success at the task and subject level. The other is persistence regarding the students' ability to stay in their studies, which requires sufficient finances, other necessary resources, enough time to devote to the effort, and sufficient wellbeing to derive satisfaction and growth from the study experience. Although one aspect is the realm of academic learning support and the other is pastoral support, there is a complex interplay between the many influences on students' abilities and motivations to persist with learning and on their decisions about whether to stay in their studies, change courses, withdraw temporarily, or leave university altogether.

Because such a wide range of often intersecting factors can influence students' efforts to persist, there is no simple answer for why some students persist through challenges and others in similar situations do not. A student's capacity to persist varies according to:

- their personality traits, dispositions, and strategies (e.g., self-confidence, attitudes and beliefs, ability to manage stress, optimistic/pessimistic mindsets, and self-efficacy)
- their motivational influences (e.g., goals, expectations, and prior achievements/success)
- their quality of engagement with learning
- the frequency and complexity of obstacles or level of challenges they encounter
- the competing demands they experience in different parts of their lives and the weighing of the relative financial, emotional, and future costs of these
- a range of other contextual factors associated with teaching/learning, the university environment, and personal circumstances
- the choices and actions they take in response to challenges (e.g., whether they seek help, resolve issues, or commit more time to tasks)
- their perceptions of and access to social, family, and/or institutional support.[74]

Student experience surveys and studies explore the influences on students' decisions to persist and those that contribute to decisions to withdraw from studies.[75] These are familiar to Indigenous support staff. Influences on Indigenous students' decisions about whether to persist or withdraw include the presence or lack of adequate finance, academic and social support, cultural isolation or discomfort, supportive peer networks and positive relationships with peers and academics, family support, identity support, a sense of belonging, and socio-emotional well-being, physical health, and disability support. Further, perceptions and experiences of racism, difficulties managing heavy workloads when juggling study, paid work, family, and other responsibilities, as well as issues associated with university services and teaching and learning environments, can affect decisions to persist or withdraw from studies.[76]

These influences on Indigenous students' decisions to persist or withdraw indicate areas of student experiences to which support staff need to be vigilant. They underline the need to understand Indigenous students' levels of preparation and their strengths, weaknesses, personal circumstances, and study conditions to provide appropriate levels and types of support.

It is important to note that students can be persistent in their academic learning efforts and still not succeed. This is the case for Indigenous students who continue studying but experience ongoing subject failures and repeat subjects, often more than once and sometimes several times. This would indicate that such students are still determined, motivated, or future goal-focused but are not receiving realistic course advice, sufficient assistance, or the particular forms of assistance they require to develop the capabilities they need to succeed. However, they are accumulating added financial debts in the process of their subsequent attempts.

Therefore, persistence is a very complex phenomenon, and assisting students to persist through various academic and personal challenges is the real work of Indigenous student support services. Everything student support staff do should work towards enabling students to persist with academic tasks and stay in their studies.

Motivation and persistence

Students need both the skills and motivation to persist with their learning when they encounter challenges. Academic motivation is a mental process that directs students to behaviours and choices that will help them achieve their academic goals. Motivation is a complex psychological construct; however, in simple terms, it can be understood as the will, energy, purposefulness or actions a student directs or takes for their learning goals. From a learning perspective, a student's level of motivation influences their commitment to a learning task, their quality of engagement with learning, their degree of effort to achieve goals, and how long they are willing to persist when they confront an obstacle.[77]

In learning situations, students' motivation levels can vary between tasks and are influenced by multiple individual and contextual factors, including emotions.[78] Individual students can also be motivated in multiple and varying ways and by different things, such as curiosity and interest in something, the usefulness, value, or benefit of an activity, bribes or rewards, or the fear of penalisation or failure.[79] It is our experience that most Indigenous students who decide to pursue higher education study are motivated by a desire to achieve career goals and more general goals such as increasing their chances of a better future, proving to themselves they can do it, being a role model for other Indigenous people, making the most of their opportunities, and being in a better position to help their community. Some of the students we interviewed reported that these broader goals reminded them of their reasons for studying and helped them persist when they encountered challenges. When asked what they did when they felt their motivation slipping, students talked about motivators and strategies for re-motivating themselves:

> Strategies that I've used would be like, 'why am I here', 'what is my objective for doing all this', and it is being there to get a degree, and I guess that's sort of the driving factor. There's a lot of other things as well, like, your family and that type of thing, but I think the sole thing would be to get a degree and to pass the course.[80]

> I do know that one of the things that really motivates me is when people tell me that I can't do it, and I just want to prove them wrong … another motivation is I am doing this for my family, and then I'm kind of sacrificing being with my family to be here, so do a good job of it.[81]

However, these broader goals were not always enough to maintain motivation at the task level. One student stated: 'I still have those other underlying motivations and reasons for what I am doing, but I think, intellectually, I have to be engaged, otherwise I … can't mentally stimulate myself to listen or apply myself.'[82] Other students discussed their motivation strategies for learning and learning tasks. These reveal the interplay between motivation and self-efficacy beliefs, interest, efforts, and peer support for different students:

> Even if it's something you don't like or are not good at … trying to do it means it becomes easier, and you think 'I can do it', and it then becomes more interesting, so you don't think negative about your learning.[83]

> [Supplementary] tutoring really helps; that's good for motivation. That's two hours of study done, even if you didn't feel like it in the first place.[84]

> I think, keep in contact with people and let them know how you are going if you are not doing so well. There is so much support here for people to talk to, even other students, you kind of bounce off each other; if you feel like you're not getting somewhere or [the] same with them, you've got each other.[85]

The scholarly literature on motivation is extensive and complex; however, it clearly demonstrates a strong correlation between motivation, achievement, persistence, the ability to regulate behaviours, and wellbeing.[86] It is not necessary to understand theoretical debates in the literature, but it is helpful to be aware of the different motivational constructs.[87] Some of this knowledge is useful for support staff to remember when considering how to respond to students who appear to have lost motivation or are not engaging sufficiently with their subject requirements, including those who engage in avoidance or procrastination behaviours that affect their achievement.

Motivation theories are applied to domains outside education; however, many studies have been conducted in educational contexts, from early education to all schooling levels and higher education.[88] Despite the academic terminology of motivation theories, most of what we discuss in this section will seem like common sense to staff who have had lots of experience supporting Indigenous students.

One strand of motivational theory is *achievement goal theory*, which encompasses the idea that students' motives for study can act as goals that motivate them to take actions that will help them achieve their goals. Goal setting has been found to assist at-risk students to overcome obstacles to their success.[89] However, studies indicate that students are more likely to influence their outcomes positively if their goals are specific to tasks; if students commit to the goal, believe they can achieve the goal, and have the skills to do so.[90] This suggests that Indigenous students' larger goals, such as those mentioned above, may help them maintain motivation but not be focused enough to help them improve their achievement outcomes. Struggling students, in particular, may benefit from setting task-oriented goals but are likely to need assistance to do so.

Another well-developed area of motivational theory is *expectancy-value theory*. This theory proposes that students' expectancy (anticipation) of achieving success and the perceived value of a learning task influences their decisions about the degree of effort they are prepared to expend for any task.[91] According to one theoretical model, students' decisions about how much effort to make are determined by a range of variables, such as their perceptions of their competence and the difficulty of the task, goals, and self-beliefs, prior experiences of learning tasks and interpretations of past performances, memories of emotions related to performance in past tasks, and surrounding social influences.[92]

Students may also value the worth of making an effort in a task according to their interest in a subject or how it relates to their future goals. Thus, a student may choose to work hard to do well in a task or subject they enjoy but choose to aim for a lower outcome in a task or subject they are not interested in but must complete because it will help them meet a longer-term goal. However, it is important to remember that while interest often stimulates more effort to do well and, therefore, aids persistence and success, a student's negative perception of their competence and degree of success or failure can negatively affect their interest in a task or subject.

Students may also choose how much effort to exert based on negative feelings about a task. For example, if a task provokes performance anxiety, a student may decide the effort to do well is not worth the cost to their health or wellbeing, and so choose to accept a lower outcome. This has implications for the support effort because it would indicate a student's need for strategies to manage their anxiety and assistance with skills and strategies to succeed in a task.

Self-efficacy theory is a theory of motivation and has been discussed in some detail in the 'Self-efficacy and academic self-efficacy' section in this chapter. While self-efficacy theory shares some similarities with expectancy theories, it is more micro-analytic regarding individuals' beliefs about their own capabilities.[93]

Attribution theories are a strand of motivational theory that have been widely applied in retention studies when institutions have tried to understand why students leave their studies. Attribution theories attempt to understand the *causes* to which students attribute their success or failure to persist and achieve desired outcomes. The perceived causes (or attributions) students use to explain their failures or successes influence their motivation.[94] Studies have shown that students are 'likely to persist in their efforts at learning when they feel in control.'[95] For example, students who attribute their achievement outcomes to causes that they have some control over, such as the degree of effort they make or finding time to study, are more likely to be motivated to persist. However, a student who attributes their achievement outcomes to something they feel they have little control over and cannot change is unlikely to believe that their efforts would greatly affect their outcomes, for example, a student who believes that the cause of a low outcome is their perceived low ability or not being smart enough or, for example, the belief of a student we interviewed that her stress responses were just part of who she was and who had never sought strategies to manage stress.

Importantly, students' attributions also have emotional effects on their future efforts. For example, a student who has made sufficient effort to achieve a good outcome is likely to feel a sense of satisfaction and be motivated to keep making the required effort the next time. The student who attributes a poor outcome to not being smart enough or being unable to manage negative thinking is more likely to feel hopeless or defeated and consider it not worth increasing their efforts or changing their strategies. These negative thoughts and feelings are likely to decrease their sense of control over their outcomes and, hence, their motivation for future similar tasks. Conversely, a student who attributes a poor achievement outcome to an insufficient effort on their part might experience it as a setback or disappointment but be more likely to increase their effort the next time because they know they could do better. Such a student would be less likely to lose motivation and more likely to persist despite having experienced a previous poor outcome.

There are multiple causes to which students might attribute their positive and negative achievement outcomes, for example, abilities, amount of effort, interest/enjoyment of a subject, dislike of a subject, the perceived value of the subject, like/dislike of the lecturer/tutor, concerns about the Indigenous content, the difficulty of a subject, good or bad luck, the presence or absence of support, health issues, and unpredictable life events. However, students often make inaccurate achievement attributions that mean that the real causes of their successes and failures are not realistically acknowledged. In some cases, this makes it more difficult for them to consider changing their approach to learning, seeking help, or developing strategies that would help them persist and improve their outcomes. Thus, how students think about the possible causes of their achievement outcomes can influence their future approaches to academic tasks and either enhance or erode their feelings of being in control of their learning.

The good news is that students can learn to make more accurate attributions regarding their achievement outcomes. This increases their chances of addressing issues they have previously assumed that they cannot control or that erode their motivation to persist with their learning.[96] Some students will need help to find more accurate explanations for their successes/failures and develop strategies for addressing the causes of their failures or low outcomes. Ways to assist a student might include providing constructive feedback on their learning approaches and study behaviours and how these might contribute to their outcomes or helping them interpret academic feedback constructively. Ideally, assistance should help students believe that their efforts can help them achieve success and motivate them to continue their efforts and that if their efforts lead to failures or fall short of their expectations, it does not necessarily reflect their ability or imply that they did not make sufficient effort; rather, it might indicate that their learning and study strategies are not effective.

Self-determination theory[97] begins with the understanding that humans have an inherent propensity to be curious and to explore, inquire, satisfy their interests, and develop their capacities. The proposition is that humans are *intrinsically motivated* (i.e., have an inherent or inner drive) to develop and thrive and are rewarded by the inner satisfaction and enjoyment of activities that increase their knowledge, competence, and mastery. However, other imperatives in their lives limit the extent to which individuals can pursue their intrinsic interests. For example, they might include early childhood socialisation towards cultural norms and values, the more controlled learning situations of formal education, and the requirement to follow workplace rules, social norms, and regulations for behaviour, all of which place individuals in learning situations that may not be intrinsically interesting or enjoyable. In this process, a different type of motivation emerges—*extrinsic motivation*. The source of extrinsic motivation might stem from the external reward of doing what is expected or doing well at something they do not greatly enjoy. Alternatively, the source might stem from a desire to avoid some form of penalty for noncompliance, for example, wanting to achieve approval through good grades, to avoid the shame or disappointment of poor grades, or for an economic or social reward, such as income or status, rather than just the satisfaction of doing a good job.[98]

Students tend to be motivated by both intrinsic and extrinsic forms of motivation because universities serve the pursuit of knowledge and education for its intrinsic rewards and self-satisfaction, as well as for more instrumental purposes such as preparing for work and its extrinsic rewards in the form of recognition of achievement, leading to future income and status. However, studies have revealed that individuals can internalise the external gains associated with learning into their own values—that is, the external rewards associated with learning achievements become internalised and integrated as the intrinsic values of the student. This often leads to an enjoyment of learning by finding it intrinsically interesting for its own sake and not just for the external rewards that it also brings.

Self-determination theorists have investigated the social and environmental factors that support or undermine intrinsic motivation to help explain the variations in an individual's motivation levels. Studies have found that satisfying three areas of human needs enables individuals to be motivated by something intrinsically interesting and enjoyable and/or to internalise external motivations to integrate them into a more self-regulated 'inner drive.' These areas are competence, autonomy, and relatedness.

An activity needs to be in the vicinity of a student's *competence* for them to gain the satisfaction and enjoyment that comes with the movement towards mastery. Not gaining satisfaction will increase the chance that their motivation will continue to be undermined. *Autonomy* does not equate to independence but to the notion of a student's freedom to exert some control over how they engage with or pursue learning activities, which supports developing a sense of their own purposefulness in learning. *Relatedness* refers to a need for security and attachment to 'supportive others' in the process of learning. Security is derived from the connectedness to those who can provide positive and constructive feedback that contributes to feelings of competence, encourages persistence in attempts to master an activity, and helps build self-confidence.[99] Studies have confirmed that feelings of competence, on their own, did not exert much influence on motivation levels unless a person's sense of autonomy was preserved (self-determination regarding their actions).[100] Self-determination theory and its conditions of competence, autonomy, and relatedness support the importance of helping students develop their skills and strategic capabilities (competence) so they can be in charge of their own learning (autonomy) and ensuring they have sufficient sources of support and constructive feedback to do this (connectedness).

In summary, from the support perspective, it is not necessary to master the academic language and terminology of these different motivational constructs or have deep knowledge of these concepts when dealing with different student dispositions and situations that affect their motivation. These theories are presented in brief to help support staff consider the range of possible sources of student motivation and possible reasons for the loss of motivation and to provide some prompts for investigating what may motivate or demotivate a student or cause them to avoid the learning and study behaviours that are important to success. We suggest that there is something to be learnt from all these theories, rather than binding one's understanding to a single theory.

There are also some useful factors to consider. A general 'front of mind' awareness of the links between motivation, achievement outcomes, and implications for wellbeing is important. It is also important to be aware of the significance of students' motivational states for their persistent engagement with learning tasks. Further, it is necessary to be mindful that some students' negative emotional states and declining levels of engagement or commitment to learning may indicate low motivational states and that these may reflect how they perceive their abilities, how they are affected by contextual issues associated with learning tasks, or other negative influences or personal situations. It is also essential to remember that students are motivated in multiple and variable ways. Students can also lose motivation for multiple reasons, and their loss of motivation manifests in varying ways and behavioural reactions that may lead to further loss of motivation. Staff should be open to exploring and helping students to resolve a range of factors that may be affecting their motivation, for example, their difficulties feeling comfortable or engaging with academic content or peers in classroom contexts, skill levels and strategies for different tasks, experiences of success/failure, interest levels in particular subjects or tasks, and finance, accommodation, and personal factors that may be affecting their ability to stay motivated and engaged in learning.

Helping students examine their situation from a different perspective can also help. Depending on the individual student, support staff can encourage demotivated students to try one or more of the following: exploring and processing more accurate causes of their outcomes, moderating their thinking about their abilities, reflecting on the decisions and choices that drive their commitment to their studies or their degree of effort, setting task-oriented and/or behaviour-oriented goals, focusing on measuring their performance against their past performance rather than others' performance, interpreting informal and formal feedback constructively, finding strategies, or seeking help to manage difficult personal situations.

While motivation can be considered a behavioural attribute of individual students, it is important to remember that classroom-learning contexts, the university environment, a student's degree of interest in their subjects, their levels of success or failure, their access to and perceptions of social and academic support, and their personal circumstances and health and wellbeing can play a role in their levels of motivation at any particular moment during their studies. Support staff can help students maintain motivation by helping them determine what is causing their demotivation and develop strategies for managing any situational, contextual, and environmental factors. They can remind students to try different strategies to discover what works best for them and assist them with suggested strategies to develop the cognitive (mental processing), metacognitive (strategic), and affective (emotional) knowledge/skills they need to succeed in tasks.

Student engagement

Students' forms and degrees of engagement with teaching, learning, and social environments at university influence their learning and achievement. The quality of engagement is also an indicator of student success.[101] Student engagement is one of those terms that seem self-explanatory. However, our exploration of the research on student success suggests the quality of students' engagement is critical for Indigenous students' achievement outcomes and influenced by a complex interplay of many individual, institutional, and external factors.[102] Further, we suggest that the quality of Indigenous students' engagement is connected to other key influences on students' ability to succeed or continue to study, including persistence, motivation, belonging and transition and the academic and peer/social interactions, financial situations and personal circumstances, and support that influence those.

While there are various definitions of student engagement, a widely used definition in Australia is 'students' involvement in activities and conditions that are linked with high-quality learning.'[103] Although the understanding of student engagement is weighted towards the student's effort, a student's degree and quality of engagement pivot on the student–institutional relationship:

> The concept of engagement embraces a specific understanding of the relationship between students and institutions. Institutions are responsible for creating environments that make learning possible, and that afford opportunities to learn. The final responsibility for learning, however, rests with students.[104]

> Engagement occurs where students feel they are part of a group of students and academics committed to learning, where learning outside the classroom is considered as important as the timetabled and structured experience, and where students actively connect to the subject matter.[105]

There is a long history of studies regarding the factors that influence or indicate students' engagement, correlate student engagement variables with student outcomes, and review the various research perspectives and models reported in the literature.[106] Engagement indicators are 'framed by a combination of interrelated physical, social cognitive and psychological dimensions' that influence 'student belonging, retention and success.'[107] There are also different research perspectives in the literature, many of which overlap.[108] Some insights are based on student surveys and self-reporting.[109] The engagement discourse is also debated and subject to critique, including its relation to the neoliberal focus on institutional and individual accountability and performativity.[110]

From our perusal of the literature, research about student engagement generally aims to inform institutional efforts to facilitate students' engagements in activities that enhance their quality of learning—the larger intention being to encourage higher rates of student success, quality outcomes, and retention. Further, like the persistence scholarship, the accumulation of international engagement research over time and across different countries and education contexts suggests that student engagement is a complex phenomenon, involving the interplay of different student, institutional and external variables, and influences that vary according to the specificities of different contexts and individual students. Therefore, what influences and/or works for one student, student cohort, or context might not work for another student, cohort, or context.

Numerous studies have confirmed that students' purposeful engagement in learning-oriented activities positively influences student success, persistence, and social engagement and the quality of their efforts.[111] Improvements to the following student outcomes have been reported: general abilities and critical thinking, practical competence and skills transferability, cognitive development, self-esteem and psychosocial development, productive racial and gender identity formations, moral and ethical development, student satisfaction, accrual of social capital, improved grades and persistence.[112]

The following influences have been linked to enhanced student engagement:

- a sufficient degree of academic challenge to keep students engaged—although for some Indigenous students, if the degree of challenge is too great, students can become overwhelmed and either engage ineffectively or disengage
- student interactions with staff, especially outside classroom learning and to meet individual needs—although for some Indigenous students, if these interactions are not positive, they may decrease engagement
- student participation in extracurricular activities associated with the university—although despite the value of recreational, ambassador, and community-oriented activities, for some Indigenous students, too much time spent on these activities can detract from time spent learning

- living on campus (possibly an outdated finding)—although accommodation, transport, and commuting time issues are known barriers for Indigenous students
- engaging or interacting with peers or others in learning communities— although if interactions with others are judgemental or threaten students' sense of self, these can have negative effects on Indigenous students' engagement
- interactions with diverse peers (enhances personal and social outcomes), which can positively or negatively affect Indigenous students.[113]

Findings also suggest that students with higher-order skills, such as analysis, critical analysis, synthesis, and evaluation skills, tend to be more engaged, although these skills do develop through deeper engagement in learning.[114] Findings confirm that academics who expect and *support* their students to achieve high standards and challenge students to extend themselves enhance student engagement. Indigenous support staff and supplementary tutors play an important role for Indigenous students in the absence of these qualities in academics or when students have difficulty accessing academics when needed. Further, how institutions encourage learners influences students' engagement, as does an institution's culture, including their response to cultural diversity and the preparation of students.[115] This would also apply to how well Indigenous student support staff encourage, prepare, and assist Indigenous learners.

Notably, studies have not established that the characteristics of students on entry (e.g., student backgrounds and prior achievements) determine the extent to which they are likely to engage. This implies that a high achieving or very capable Indigenous student is not more or less likely to engage more deeply in learning than an underprepared Indigenous student. However, studies have shown that 'students who are least prepared academically benefit more from engagement than those who are most prepared, in terms of [the] effect on grades and persistence.'[116] This suggests that engagement is critical for underprepared students' chances of success and that support staff must be alert to signs of student disengagement, such as low attendance and reluctant participation in peer learning activities. Further, studies have confirmed that a successful transition into higher education is a prerequisite for ongoing engagement, reflected in developing an 'identity as a student' and a sense of belonging to the university community.[117] This has implications for the design of Indigenous student support strategies.

The higher education literature also discusses student *disengagement*, inertia, and negative engagement experiences, which will be very familiar to Indigenous student support staff.[118] In the US context, for example, studies have revealed that some student cohorts (e.g., international; racial minorities; disabled; lesbian, gay, bisexual, transgender and queer orientations; low socio-economic status; first-in-family; part-time; commuter; and transfer students) are more likely to experience engagement negatively. Such students may be highly engaged but feel overwhelmed, isolated, or alienated in those engagements.[119] Negative engagements are well reported in the Indigenous higher education literature, and the cultural safety and competency discourses and agendas are a response to Indigenous students' negative experiences of engagement in learning and other areas of the university. Given the complexity of factors that can affect the quality of students' engagement, these broader strategies are not sufficient for assisting students experiencing difficulties in engaging in the learning and social environments of the university.

Further, Indigenous students reported higher levels of engagement in the *Australasian Survey of Student Engagement 2009 Institution Report*[120] and expressed similar satisfaction with university experiences, similar levels of engagement in learning activities, and higher general skills outcomes to non-Indigenous students despite much lower retention and completion rates than other students.[121] Of interest to support staff is that Indigenous students reported that the university provided a more supportive learning environment than their non-Indigenous peers. However, they reported less institutional support for non-academic responsibilities than non-Indigenous students. The former may reflect the presence of Indigenous support provisions and the latter the challenging circumstances under which many Indigenous students study, which university services or staff may not understand or make allowances for. This analysis of Indigenous student survey responses was cautious regarding the implications, underlying details, and within-in-group differences among Indigenous cohorts, and it is now quite dated. Nevertheless, it cautions against assuming that Indigenous students' engagements are necessarily perceived negatively by them or lead to quality outcomes.

Insights from the engagement literature have implications for Indigenous support practices, most notably, the importance of monitoring student progress to track variables related to their engagement. These variables include academic, institutional, and external factors and influences. Attendance and students' interactions with learning management systems are the most accessible indicators of student engagement. However, the qualitative aspects of learning that are not so easy to track are equally important, such as interest in learning, time and effort on tasks, the development of cognitive, metacognitive, and affective capabilities and skill levels, improvements in learning outcomes, positive interactions with peers, tutors, and academics, and social engagements related to learning. These qualitative aspects indicate that support staff need to be in contact with students to know how they are tracking. Significantly, a positive transition experience is a requirement for ongoing engagement. This implies that students' strengths and challenge areas and their capacities to engage must be considered from very early on in their commencing semester so that the indicated level of support can be provided.

The correlation between students' levels of learning and social engagements and their outcomes also implies the need to investigate the level, quality, and forms of engagement of students who have low outcomes to discern what might affect their ability to engage in activities that lead to higher quality learning. Many factors can affect a student's ability to engage or achieve successful outcomes, and these should be explored for less engaged or disengaged students. For example, a recent Australian study reported that if students felt they did not fit in or felt disconnected in classroom interactions, this influenced decisions about whether to attend classes.[122] Support staff can do much to assist students in these cases through suggestions and practical strategies.

Although there is an established correlation between levels of engagement and outcomes, it is important not to draw a direct causal link between low outcomes and engagement levels. Some highly engaged students achieve low outcomes. Further, it is important to remember that it is difficult to gauge students' levels of engagement from observations of their behaviours. Some engaged students may act as if they are not engaged when they are, and others may participate in ways in which they appear to be engaged but are not very engaged at all.[123]

Perhaps the following student quote confirms just how important the experience of achieving success and developing confidence in one's ability is for classroom and peer engagement and a student's self-efficacy beliefs and sense of belonging. The implications for student support staff are stark:

> I didn't go to my unit tutorials ... I was so embarrassed to go. I just didn't go for a whole year ... I went once or twice, but it was like you go there, and you sit in the corner of the classroom, and you kind of feel more dumb than when you walked in because you're not actually engaging, you are too embarrassed to engage, and you just sit there for a whole hour ... A lot of students ... say that they are too shame to go in and it's embarrassing. But it comes along with the confidence, and then once they understand they are doing good from their tutor and start getting some good marks back, then they start to go.[124]

This student was attending their supplementary tutorial sessions and was motivated to learn. Without engagement with these one-on-one tutors, her outcomes may well have been withdrawal from her studies.

Self-organisation and study behaviours

A student's ability to organise their time and routines to maintain their attendance levels, assessments, study progress, and revision loads is critical to their ability to meet their academic demands while simultaneously managing other aspects of their lives. Self-organisation is a component of self-regulated learning and is generally discussed as part of that literature. We have given it a separate section of its own because it relates to students' efforts to succeed and staff efforts to assist students. In our experience, many students take a long time to take control of this area of effort and many support staff underestimate the knowledge, skills, and capacities of students to do this without some quite specific guidance. Simply issuing students a semester calendar and telling them to plan their timetables and study hard is insufficient for many students. While this is an area where students often share and learn from each other, in our experience, many Indigenous students, including academically able students, do not grasp these skills. This is also an area where university learning centres provide workshops but where many Indigenous students, for a range of reasons, are not confident enough or inclined to register and attend.

From our academic persistence study, we learnt that it is common for students to need quite specific assistance in the following areas:[125]

- systems for semester calendars, for example, colour-coding so they can easily see the lecture, tutorial, supplementary tutoring, and assessment times and dates for each subject
- systems for weekly plans for organising study and other essential activities (i.e., lecture times, the entry of times for assessment preparation, their supplementary tutor appointments, any preparation tasks for tutorial and supplementary tutoring sessions, their employment shifts and other regular recreation, and family or community commitments)
- the ability to interpret course outlines and the meaning of assessment rubrics to determine what sort of weekly preparation is expected and what the mark weightings might indicate for the effort expected of students for different tasks or subjects
- knowledge about how long a learning or assessment task is likely to take (e.g., how long to schedule for an academic reading, weekly science or maths exercises, research, note-taking, or drafting of assignments)
- systems and strategies for taking effective notes from lectures, academic articles, and texts, as well as systems for organising study notes for weekly and study period revision purposes
- knowledge, skills, and strategies for study and exam preparation
- knowledge and skills for using learning management and library and information systems
- knowledge, skills, and strategies for managing negative or unproductive behaviours, (e.g., recognising why and developing strategies for managing procrastination, avoidance behaviours, and other behavioural or emotional responses that demotivate or derail students' efforts, such as anxiety, stress, frustration, anger, dislike for a lecturer, lack of interest in a subject, difficulties in teaching classrooms, and peer interactions)
- strategies for managing unexpected events in students' academic and personal lives that derail their plans to enable them to catch up with their studies as early as possible
- communication skills for negotiating directly with lecturers or tutors when students cannot meet a compulsory obligation (e.g., arriving on time, meeting a deadline, participating in a learning activity, or asking for help)
- negotiation skills for establishing agreed plans involving student administrative requirements (e.g., issues associated with students' academic progression or completion time)
- knowledge of university policies, regulations, and processes related to students' results and subsequent decisions (e.g., special consideration and appeals processes).

These are important sets of knowledge, skills, and behaviours students must learn to study efficiently and effectively and recover when they fall behind or go off track for any reason. Students will always become disorganised from time to time; however, knowing *how* to be organised and *how* to get back on track is critical to their chances of success.

How students organise themselves and keep on top of academic and other demands on their time is a highly individual factor—what works for one student might not work for another, and what is useful for students in one discipline may not be so useful for students in another discipline. For example, we learnt from our student interviews that some students need a steady routine to keep up with their loads and prevent anxiety and stress from reaching unproductive levels. Other students argue they work much more efficiently under pressure, and certainly, some do. However, this should always be checked against students' outcomes because it can be a rationale for leaving tasks to the last minute or indicate that a student does not know how to organise themselves or is struggling to find a workable routine. Nevertheless, it is important to recognise that a degree of stress is productive and that stress can be a strong motivator for intensive application to a study task. However, the tolerance for stress before it becomes unproductive or debilitating varies widely among students.

Another difficulty for students is that they do not always fully understand that it takes time to determine what sort of self-organisation systems, study routines, and behaviours are most effective and that they can adjust and refine other people's suggestions to suit their own needs. It is beneficial to explain these things to students and provide examples of effective systems for managing their time, tasks, learning resources and notes. Students with heavy carer or employment loads or employment that involves irregular shifts may benefit from suggestions about how others manage their study routines, as may external students who have less engagement with peers. This implies that support staff should not take students' knowledge, skills, and capacities in this area for granted.

We also suggest that staff audit any relevant university academic skills workshops to assess whether they are likely to meet the needs of underprepared Indigenous students. Especially for Indigenous students with English as a second language, the pace of workshops and assumed prior educational experience, knowledge, and skills level should be considered. The quality of these sessions can vary widely across universities; thus, it is useful to examine a range of university websites to understand the advice given in these areas. If a university's workshops are considered helpful, Indigenous students should be encouraged to use them; however, it should not be assumed that students do, nor should students' needs in these areas be ignored if they have not attended these workshops on their own initiative. Similarly, audits and assessments of online resources and videos that can be useful for students in these areas are necessary, because these also vary widely in quality, relevance, and usefulness. For example, some YouTube videos about note-taking systems fail to highlight the real purpose of keeping organised notes by leaning towards product advertisements and polished examples that suggest unattainable standards. Nevertheless, some of these contain useful ideas that support staff can provide to students. Any YouTube video requires careful assessment to ensure it is suitable before being posted as a student resource.

Support staff have various options for attempting to meet student needs in this area, including working individually with students, devising group sessions on a selected area for Indigenous students only, providing a list of evaluated online resources that might be useful, and encouraging students to attend university skills sessions if these are considered helpful but always following up that students learn what they needed from them. Supplementary tutors can also be a source of knowledge for students about how to stay organised.

Commencing students need assistance in these areas very early during their studies, ideally beginning in the orientation week and through the first few weeks, with continued follow-up until they are managing well. For example, many Indigenous students revising for exams, including those who take open-book exams, would achieve better results if given early guidance and systems for compiling and keeping their notes organised throughout the semester instead of rushing around during the exam study period to borrow from and share notes with others. The study period should ideally be used for familiarising and practising how to use the content of their notes to answer anticipated questions. This last-minute rush was particularly mentioned by the law students we interviewed.

Student belonging

The concept of belonging refers to students' psychosocial sense of being accepted, valued, included, and supported in their interactions with peers, academics, and others in both formal and informal learning and social environments of the university.[126] That is, belonging refers to students' sense of their place in the university—how they fit into the academic and social environment of the university, how at home and connected to others they feel, and the feeling they are part of and valued by others in the university community. A sense of belonging is a supportive influence in the face of challenges and, thus, an enabler of persistence, engagement, and achievement.[127]

Indigenous students expressed, in straightforward ways, their initial doubts about whether they belonged, for example, 'I felt like a fish out of water.'[128] However, Indigenous students also expressed doubts about how they fitted in, highlighting their awareness of their educational position in relation to other students. The following quote provides such an example: 'I wasn't sure if I was smart enough, if I was worth being here. There were times when I thought, "do I really belong here?" even though I really want to be here.'[129]

As every student support officer would be well aware from experience, the research on belonging confirms that it is too simplistic to understand a student's sense of belonging as an individual's subjective response to the university environment.[130] Rather, feelings of belonging are 'directly shaped by the broader campus climate and the perceptions of belonging that students derive from their daily interactions with other students, faculty, staff and administrators on campus and the messages those interactions convey about their belonging.'[131]

The concept of student belonging has been a persistent theme in the international higher education retention literature. The facilitation of students' sense of belonging was initially conceptualised in terms of students' *integration* into the academic and social environments of their chosen university and discipline.[132] However, insights into students' feelings of belonging and the factors that influence these feelings have developed over the decades.[133] Over time, researchers have investigated different contributors to feelings of belonging or not belonging to provide either more nuanced and complex accounts of what influences students' sense of belonging or to provide more empirical evidence for what enhances student belonging.[134]

Much of this research has emerged in response to increases in student diversity. Various aspects of academic and social engagement that appear to support students' sense of belonging have been investigated. These include the importance of making friends at university as a form of informal social, emotional, and academic support, positive formal and informal interactions with fellow students and academic staff through classroom and other learning experiences, positive attachment to their future profession or occupation (e.g., work experience opportunities or closer attention to placement experiences), identification with their disciplines, and positive interactions with fellow students in the social activities or environment of the university.[135]

Although research has continuously confirmed that students' academic and social engagements in universities are central to developing a sense of belonging, scholars have argued that 'it is not engagement per se that drives a sense of belonging, as it is students' perceptions of their belonging that derives from their engagements.'[136] Therefore, belonging is increasingly being understood as multidimensional, with students' sense of belonging becoming one more factor in a complex interplay of individual, institutional, and external influences that affect students' feelings of satisfaction with study and their decisions to stay or depart from their studies. Thus, efforts to support students' feelings of belonging increasingly form part of the array of institutional efforts intended to support students' transition experiences, engagement, persistence, and success. IEUs' efforts to provide environments that engender students' sense of belonging need to be considered a part of the wider institutional effort. This means ensuring that IEUs' student support strategies and practices are welcoming places for all Indigenous students, signalled by the design of study spaces, the way staff and students care for and share these spaces, and friendly, interested, and helpful dispositions of staff to all students. It also means that support strategies should help students take their place in university classrooms and feel at home alongside their student peers and academics in social and learning environments. An important element of this support is learning support so that students experience success and feel equal with other students. As one student we interviewed said:

> I now feel more like a medical student, but it took a long time to get into the feel of 'ok, I am actually on the same level as all these other people' ... Once you start doing well in exams, that really helped me a lot.[137]

This aspect of some students' experiences has been conceptualised in terms of students' perceptions of their capabilities and competence levels and the relation between students' capabilities and forms of self-identification and belonging.[138] These three student perceptions—belonging, capability, and identity—are interconnected:

> Sensibilities of belonging are formed in relation to constructions of capability; to belong in a field such as higher education, the student must be recognised as having the capability to belong.[139]

Capability is deeply entwined with identity formations produced within, across and between different social contexts and spaces.[140]

Identities are complex and intersecting, not homogenous groupings.[141]

It has been argued that students who are recognised as capable can perceive themselves as capable in the eyes of others in the academy and institution. Such students are more likely to develop a sense of belonging, membership, and identification with their university and relevant sub-communities connected to their learning and university experience.[142] These groups might include their disciplinary and subject peer cohorts, learning/study communities, peer friendship groups, sporting teams, and other student groups or societies.[143] Through these memberships, the development of a sense of belonging might involve more complex forms of self-identification, for example, as a university student (e.g., identification with fellow students, their university, or graduates of higher education) or with a discipline (e.g., as a law, medical, nursing, social work, or business student). These student or learner identities denote more complex forms of self-identification, reflecting a student's self-growth and development through learning.

Students who feel that their capabilities are recognised and who feel recognised by and connected to others on a similar journey are more likely to experience a sense of belonging.[144] However, support staff need to remember that students' membership in subgroups is often for particular and transitory purposes, such as for learning, study, collaborations, recreational, or accommodation purposes, and, thus, identification with others is fluid, shifting, and always developing and changing over time. Importantly, the formation of more complex and layered identities is not necessarily a sign of shifting cultural values or the overwriting of primary identities (e.g., Aboriginal or Torres Strait Islander identities) but a sign of students incorporating understandings of 'what they do' and 'what they are in the process of becoming' into their self-understandings of 'who they are'. One medical student who had entered the clinical stage of his degree explained:

> Before, you still felt like, 'I'm just a student.' You still are a student, but you actually feel like you are involved in something, and you can actually see 'this is where I'm going,' so you are transitioning from feeling like a student to feeling more like you are actually doing something.[145]

Another medical student undergoing clinical training stated: 'you start to feel like you are actually, like, you become a doctor.'[146] Developing learner, student, and discipline identities is important preparation for assuming a future professional identity, such as a doctor, lawyer, allied health worker, nurse, social worker, engineer, teacher, or scientist. A sense of belonging to and membership in their chosen profession is important for establishing a secure professional identity.[147]

Identifying with other students based on shared experiences of higher education and finding recognition and a sense of belonging through their engagements in academic and social activities is by no means a given for Indigenous higher education students. It is also not without inner conflicts and tensions for some Indigenous students.

There are two major complicating factors for Indigenous students. The first is higher education's particular construction of commencement capability in terms of emphasising prior educational achievements.[148] This can amplify feelings of being out of place and can also engender feelings of being undeserving of a place in the university. This construction positions Indigenous students as 'less capable than others' through the discourse of under-preparedness and the array of equity provisions designed to support them. These discourses have stimulated institutional responses that include the provision of pathways and enabling programs, alternative admissions processes, identified support strategies and centres, and access to supplementary tutoring, all of which *positively influence* student success but cause other effects for some students. For example, Indigenous students, particularly those studying medicine and law, have reported 'imposter' feelings. 'Imposter syndrome' induces feelings in some students that they are merely masquerading as university students or that other students are the real students, and they are merely observers because they enter with lower scores than their peers.[149] One first-year student who had been admitted through an alternative entry scheme explained:

> I felt … the first few weeks that I was kind of like the … invader or something like that, just coming in through the Indigenous way. But as I have gone on and feel I can answer and do things … basically, I feel like I am on the same level as them.[150]

This implies that Indigenous support staff need to consider alternative selection processes seriously so they can explicitly inform all Indigenous students that they have been through a formal alternative selection process, that faculty and IEU staff have assessed them and consider them to have a good chance of succeeding, that they will be given sufficient support to do so, and that they have earned their place in the university. This provides an important source for students' self-messaging—a technique the medical student we interviewed said he relied on until he felt he was doing just as well as other students and, therefore, could think of himself as one of them. The selection processes this student had gone through enabled him to construct a positive narrative about his abilities to learn and succeed—an accurate narrative he used for positive self-messaging to counter self-doubt and the feeling of being out of place during the early stages of his studies.

Being successful in subject assessments and proving to themselves that they can improve their results increases students' beliefs in their capabilities, enabling them to assume a student identity associated with their discipline. The students we interviewed related some poignant moments in which they realised they were students of their discipline. For example, an arts/business student watching a business report on the nightly news realised he understood everything that was being said and, at that moment, felt he could think of himself as a business student. Previously, he considered himself more of an arts student because he had not felt at home in his business course or among his business peers. In another example, a law student assisting a friend with a car purchase suddenly realised she was scrutinising the contract like a lawyer. Reaching this realisation can take some time—the business student was in his second year, and the law student was in her third year and there is no guarantee that all students will have epiphanies such as those mentioned. However, the self-realisation of themselves as capable students who are engaged in the process of settling into their student or discipline identities should be considered part of a successful transition for Indigenous students and key to a feeling of belonging.

The second complicating factor that affects Indigenous students' sense of belonging and sometimes influences their decisions to withdraw is the construction of Indigenous Australians as 'other' in academic knowledge and culture. The academic and cultural bias underpinning the misrepresentation, omission, and mistreatment of Indigenous Australian knowledge, experiences, perspectives, circumstances, and issues in university courses has been reported as problematic for Indigenous students; however, some studies have also found this not to be an issue for some students.[151] Likewise, some assume that all Indigenous students are authoritative reference points in classroom discussions about Indigenous issues, drawing unwanted attention to some students.[152] These examples of positioning regarding knowledge can engender additional feelings in students of being spotlighted, misrecognised, or misunderstood as members of their Aboriginal and Torres Strait Islander communities and as individuals. Either or both of these factors can cause negative experiences of academic and social engagements with academics, academic content, and peers. The effect is to undermine students' sense of belonging and ability to engage in learning interactions on their own terms and in their own interests. However, it should not be assumed that these tensions affect all students or affect them in the same ways.[153]

A sense of discomfort and feelings of not belonging can manifest in different ways for different individuals, for example, alienation (feeling unrecognised or misunderstood by the institution, its knowledge and social practices); isolation and feeling disconnected from others in academic and social environments; loneliness and general unhappiness with the experience of university; dissatisfaction with courses, staff, and the university environment; difficulties with or withdrawal from academic and social engagements; and a range of negative emotions such as anxiety, self-doubt, stress, anger, depressed moods, and diminishing confidence. As Indigenous student support staff know from experience, it is common for Indigenous students, especially commencing students, to contend with these feelings of 'not belonging' or feeling 'out of place' and the anxieties that accompany these feelings. Finding their place takes time and support—academic, social, and, in some cases, cultural support.

Belonging is an important cultural concept in many Indigenous cultures, and the links between place, people, relatedness, and connectedness are well understood in many Indigenous community contexts. Indigenous support staff have a vital role in supporting students to build their confidence in their own capabilities to engage with their non-Indigenous peers and academic learning to enable them to feel a sense of belonging and of being part of the university and disciplines in which they study. Another important source of support for managing these issues is connections to Indigenous peers. The IEU has an important role as a source of peer support, which several mature-age female students mentioned in interviews. The following is a good representation:

> Coming to [the support centre] and finding other people that are like-minded to explore our identity and how we fit into society, I think has been the biggest thing for my personal development ... But in the sense of my own identity, I've become stronger as an Aboriginal person but also stronger as a woman and what's expected of a woman and what we can achieve.[154]

For Indigenous students and staff in universities, a familiar tension arises around the degree to which the institution should accommodate the difference/diversity of Indigenous students' need to feel they belong and are accepted and valued and the degree to which students should be expected to adjust, 'fit in,' and become members of, and identify with, the university or relevant sub-communities of students.[155] The broader Indigenous institutional strategic agenda is responsible for the institutional accommodation of Indigenous concerns in this regard. Support staff are responsible for helping students find their place in the academic and social environments of the university. Indigenous student support centres have long provided a refuge where students can feel safe and a sense of belonging by being part of the Indigenous peer community and being understood by Indigenous staff and Elders. One student stated:

> I think it really helps you knowing that there is a place for Indigenous people at the university. Even having the older students there, it is just reassuring to see if people who have gone through the same things can do it, then so can I.[156]

However, Indigenous students also need a sense of belonging and place within the university's social and learning environments to engage in quality learning experiences. As well, it has been anecdotally reported that not all Indigenous students feel recognised or 'at home' in Indigenous support centres, which implies managers and staff must consider how they ensure students who need assistance actually feel at home there. It is also important to remember that students vary in their need to feel a sense of belonging or connectedness to others, which implies that support staff need to be mindful of their assumptions about individual students and their support interventions.

Indigenous knowledge and perspectives in academic learning

Issues concerning Indigenous knowledge, perspectives, and content in academic learning can be troubling or frustrating for some Indigenous students. For example, a media student who described an incident in a third-year subject said she was 'very emotionally invested' in Indigenous issues and that a lecturer deflected her concerns about the absence of Indigenous perspectives in a tutorial. While talking about the effects on her, she reported a tendency 'to get teary in class ... It's frustrating that this is Australia's history, and it continues to be denied. They don't see it.' Although it affected her emotionally, this student did not allow it to affect her learning. However, for many students, situations like this can affect their engagements and interactions with their lecturers, tutors, and non-Indigenous peers, their sense of belonging and identity, their motivation and persistence in their studies, and their emotional wellbeing.[157]

Indigenous students and Indigenous support staff have little control over curriculum issues and whether or how competently courses include Indigenous knowledge positions, content, or perspectives or how well academics manage classroom discussions about Indigenous Australian people and issues. While support staff can interact with academics about a specific issue that has negatively affected a student, they have little influence over the larger curricula issues regarding Indigenous knowledge and perspectives. Conversations about embedding Indigenous knowledge and perspectives across disciplines, the articulation of Indigenous studies subjects to degree programs, and the cultural competency of academics are in the realm of teaching and learning units, Indigenous and non-Indigenous academics, and senior Indigenous staff. The role of student support is to assist students who experience troubling encounters regarding the inclusion, omission, treatment, or misrepresentation of Indigenous knowledge, experiences, and perspectives.

A broad strategy for alienated, unsettled, angry, or frustrated students might be to encourage them to think of themselves as engaged in the process of navigating and negotiating different sets of contested knowledge and values and that this process will likely continue into their professional lives without a clear endpoint for resolving the tensions that emerge in their interactions with others.[158] Staff might help students manage any tensions and conflicts by encouraging them to think of the navigation process as a way to build language and skills that will be useful preparation for their future professional or workplace roles. The more skills and confidence students gain for shifting back and forth as they navigate the tensions between their own Indigenous knowledge perspectives and those of their disciplines or non-Indigenous peers, the better prepared for their professional lives they will be, given that this process of moving in and out of different communities of practice is likely to be lifelong. In this way, students can begin to understand their experiences as learning tools that aid their self-understanding, relations with their disciplines and future profession, and their general understanding of the Indigenous position as viewed by others. Reflective writing about their learning experiences was mentioned by one student we interviewed. Another staff strategy might be to encourage students to reflect on their experiences in this navigation and negotiation process and talk to their Indigenous peers or older Indigenous students or academics regarding ideas and strategies to help them work through their frustrations.

There are other positive and productive ways for Indigenous student support staff to guide students in this process. First, it is useful for students to remember that all students, not just Indigenous students, must navigate, negotiate, and realign, to some extent, the academic knowledge they are engaging with against what they already believe, know, and understand about the world and how they have come to know it. That is, the lenses through which students come to know and understand the world are becoming multifocal, revealing deeper questions about knowledge standpoints and methods of knowledge production. Thus, Indigenous students are well-positioned to know more about the human experience than others in their classes because many can access alternative knowledge perspectives, discourses, and experiences associated with being Aboriginal or Torres Strait Islander or both. This can be considered a strength and an advantage; however, we caution that this should not be automatically assumed for all Indigenous students. Further, to take advantage of their own knowledge, experiences, or perspectives, many Indigenous students will need assistance regarding language, skills, and strategies for incorporating and synthesising these into their academic work and class discussions. In our experience, some also need reassurance that it is okay to do this. Support staff have a role in reassuring students and helping them process their experiences.

Second, mastering a discipline involves developing the skills of critical reading, analysis, synthesis, and evaluation of different positions, from which propositions may be questioned and alternative propositions may be developed. Thus, the more deeply engaged Indigenous students are in their learning, the more likely they are to develop these skills and more complex positions about Indigenous–Western knowledge relations. Knowing how others think and view the world provides a platform to critique, counter position, and engage in more complex forms of analysis from the Indigenous perspective. Thus, what other students might consider a generic set of academic skills, Indigenous students (and other marginalised students) might perceive as a strategic skill set that can assist them to work with and against different theories and practices that affect how Indigenous realities are understood and engaged with. These strategic skills will be essential for future lives in the intersections between professional and community practices and contexts.[159] This reinforces the need to provide effective support for students to enable them to develop the sets of strategic skills and capabilities they need to master a discipline. Indigenous critique and new knowledge production are impoverished if academic meanings/content are not fully engaged and mastered.

Third, another positive way to understand the complex positioning of Indigenous students is to acknowledge that students' entry into and mastery of a discipline enables them to engage a new community, which will be important for their professional lives. These communities might be the formal academic community, more informal peer learning communities, or friendship communities, all of which can boost their confidence in expressing themselves and being accepted as themselves. Therefore, learning at university provides opportunities to develop and practice important skill sets students will need to feel a sense of competency, visibility, and belonging in the professional world.

Fourth, students who may feel anxious that academic learning is changing the way they think about their world, and who experience conflicts that threaten their sense of who they are and where they belong, can be encouraged to think in terms of adding layers to their Indigenous identity. This might mean having a more complex understanding of who they are or who they are becoming as they adopt a student or learner identity in their way to identifying as an Indigenous professional and perceiving themselves as a member of two communities of practice. Some of the students we interviewed were quite articulate in this regard, for example:

I definitely notice, you know, some Aboriginal people do have the view that when you do go to university, you are losing out on your culture or something like that, but that's not how I see it. I see it as just you are adding more onto who you are; you are gaining; you are not really losing anything. So, I'd definitely say that belonging to both sort[s] of communities, it isn't like detrimental in any way; in fact, it's helpful to me.

I find that it's good to know that we don't have to leave our identity behind in order to learn … I can't believe how important identity is to learning. That when you are told to be critical, that it's you bringing yourself and your experiences to your learning.[160]

These tensions are more problematic for some Indigenous students than others. Thus, care must be taken about assuming how these issues affect individual students and being aware of the diversity of responses in the total cohort. It must be recognised that a simple distinction based on the differences between Indigenous and non-Indigenous students is no longer an adequate basis for understanding Indigenous students' goals, challenges, and support needs in this area. For Indigenous students, the higher education pathway involves building on and expanding their knowledge perspectives and skills, situating and adjusting their behaviours and outlooks, and undertaking complex identity work as they weave student and future professional identities into the fabric of their Indigenous identities. Although many Indigenous students have shared experiences on this pathway, the experience is an individual and developmental one in which students' views shift and change as they develop and grow in response to their goals, challenges, and needs. All Indigenous students need to be supported whichever way they negotiate their learning and identities within these tensions.

Some analyses have highlighted that Indigenous knowledge and curricular content issues do not trouble all students.[161] Our interviews with students also revealed that most did not expect much attention to Indigenous knowledge or content in their courses, either because their courses did not lend themselves to it or because they understood the university was a place to study Western knowledge. This is not to say that students were unaware of omissions, bias, or the limited treatment of relevant Indigenous knowledge or content or did not think their courses should include more. They made numerous comments in this regard. They also seemed to understand why Indigenous knowledge and perspectives did not appear more in their courses and that they had to think about their own Indigenous experiences and knowledge while focusing on the discipline content they were expected to master.

Nevertheless, the students we interviewed appreciated course content that was relevant to Indigenous experiences. For example, a criminology student (from a regional city with major Indigenous youth and police conflicts) was surprised and affirmed to discover that the concept of biased policing was an area of academic research and discussion and amazed that non-Indigenous people were even aware that it occurred. An environmental science student was surprised by references to Indigenous knowledge in his course. While stating that he came to the university to understand Western science, he valued the references to Indigenous knowledge because it kept the relations between scientific and Indigenous knowledge in the front of his mind—relations that he was particularly interested in but had not expected to engage in his degree. During the first year of his law degree, this same student commented on the limits of Australian law and, in particular, the bias in its logic regarding Indigenous law and justice issues. This increased his motivation to understand how the law works and, thus, his engagement with his learning.

Another area that poses challenges for Indigenous students is uncertainty about whether it is acceptable and how to use their own experiences as an Indigenous person to augment or contest the analytical positions or arguments in texts, discussions, oral presentations, or essays. When students are uncertain or hesitant, they can be encouraged to negotiate with their lecturer and be given assistance if they need help to prepare for a negotiation. When students are unsure how to synthesise their knowledge positions into their analysis, supplementary tutors or academics are a valuable source of help if students can articulate this need for assistance.

A further challenge for students in Indigenous studies subjects or subjects that cover issues regarding Indigenous people or content is the assumption that Indigenous students are the bearers of Indigenous knowledge and well-informed on all Indigenous issues or perspectives. Indigenous students have individual responses to the expectation that they will educate others. While many Indigenous students have knowledge and experience that helps convey Indigenous perspectives and standpoints, not all do, especially younger students who have not grown up in community settings, some of whom are descendants of the Stolen Generations. Further, students' personalities influence how they engage in classroom environments. As we discovered in our interviews with students, some are forthright and committed to correcting non-Indigenous students' understandings, and others are reticent to speak up, sometimes for fear of losing control of their emotions, others for not wanting to upset the other students, and some because they cannot find the language to explain their unease.

In these circumstances, much depends on the lecturer or tutor to manage different perspectives and conversations. However, support staff also have a role. If a student is silent because they do not feel confident entering difficult discussions, do not want to upset other students, or are worried about losing control of their emotions, they can be encouraged to consider classroom discussions as opportunities to practise having difficult conversations in preparation for their working lives. They will benefit from the sharing of strategies and language skills for doing this. Support staff can learn helpful strategies by talking to other support staff, Indigenous academics, and Indigenous students for insights into the different approaches or strategies individual students use to manage uncomfortable conversations. In general, students' decisions about educating others should be respected and supported. One student who was committed to correcting other students' understanding of Indigenous issues explained how she developed constructive skills for doing this:

> [It's] taken a while to get from angry black women to articulating myself in a way that people understand … I've learnt a lot in my degree to be able to understand their position; to understand their worldview. So, when someone's saying something I think is wrong, I take a step back for a second and think about where they are coming from and their position and how to respond to that in a way to speak to how they understand things.[162]

Another more ambivalent student had a different position:

> There are some people who are uneducated and want to be educated, and that's ... fine with me. But there's others that just have no idea, and I struggle with that, and I tend to just walk away and not say anything; it's just not worth my time and energy. I'm here to study and have a degree, not to worry about all these people and their ignorant views.[163]

For another student, discussions that conflicted with her own knowledge of Indigenous experiences were very difficult, and she chose not to engage at all:

> I would just be quiet, or I would say what the majority of the class would rather hear, as opposed to what I really felt about it, just so as to not upset the class ... It was challenging because of my anger and just having to put that completely aside and just try and look at it from a different perspective ... I know it's about challenging ideas, and that's what we're supposed to do, but it was just strange, it was new, it's still new.[164]

None of this discussion suggests that the issues of Indigenous knowledge, perspectives, and content in university curricula or how academics manage the tensions that occur for Indigenous students in their subjects and courses is not an important whole-of-university issue that continues to require serious work. It is to say that current students cannot wait for the institution to adjust and accommodate and that some students' engagement, persistence, success, sense of belonging, and emotional wellbeing can be better maintained if they can develop useful management strategies.

Resilience

Resilience is a concept that circulates in Indigenous discourse and is considered an important characteristic to nurture in those who encounter adversity and setbacks. This section draws on some of the general research literature and current work in the higher education sector to exemplify how resilience develops and how it can be developed or supported in the higher education context.

There is no agreed-upon definition of resilience; however, for our purposes, resilience can be understood as an individual student's capacity to keep functioning positively through adverse circumstances or after experiencing an adverse event.[165] This idea of functioning positively either 'after' or 'through' an adverse event recognises that for many individuals, including Indigenous students, adversity can be an *acute* event that ends relatively quickly (e.g., a task or subject failure) or *chronic*, continuing for a length of time or ongoing (e.g., financial hardship, relationship and family situations, or an illness). The difference between these notions of adversity has some relevance for assisting students. Acute adverse events suggest resilience is a matter of students recovering from or learning to 'bounce back' from a setback and returning to a frame of mind that enables them to stay positive and persist with their studies. Chronic adversity suggests these students are more likely to need assistance to develop more sustained strategies for managing study demands amid adversities that are likely to recur or have no clear endpoint. From our experiences, a significant proportion of Indigenous students in universities either study while enduring constant challenges and/or live with continuous adversity or uncertainty. This suggests a need for different responses regarding staff time, coping strategies for individual students, referrals to qualified experts, and staff follow-ups to ensure strategies have been helpful.

There is a large amount of literature on resilience, which ranges across different disciplines. The concept of resilience is discussed concerning vulnerable people in adverse circumstances who are considered at risk of negative outcomes. Therefore, it is explored in the social and medical sciences, for example, psychology, social work, and psychiatry. Resilience theory has also been applied to vulnerable populations and crises in various contexts, including human poverty, community development, human and environmental disasters, and climate and environmental changes.[166]

Resilience theorists are interested in why some people in adverse circumstances experience negative outcomes and others do not. Researchers are also interested in the differences among people who experience better than expected outcomes, for example, why some individuals keep functioning well in the face of adversity, why others falter but quickly recover, and why others appear to increase their levels of adaptation to their circumstances. This interest has led to understanding human resilience in terms of the human response to self-organise, adapt, and transform to survive when encountering adversities or crises.[167]

Resilience research has also produced knowledge about resilience in terms of an individual *state of being* 'resilient' and as a *process* with links between adversity, mediating factors, and outcomes.[168] In the student support context, for instance, students' levels of self-efficacy beliefs, personal attributes, competency levels, and levels of assistance they receive from support networks or support staff are likely to be mediating factors for whether students recover from or cope with setbacks or adversity. From this perspective, resilience is considered an outcome of the interrelation between individual and environmental factors and the exchanges between individuals and others in these interrelations.

Resilience studies have also confirmed that resilience is not an inherent characteristic of individuals but is highly relational and *develops* in individuals 'within networks of social networks with family, friends, school, colleagues and neighbourhoods.'[169] The development of resilience ideally starts in childhood, but many factors can interfere with this development from childhood through to adulthood and affect a person's ability to recover from or cope with adverse events. Social support is understood to be key to developing resilience strategies.[170] The relational aspect of resilience sits well with Indigenous understandings of resilience, which are positioned within Indigenous concepts of socio-emotional wellbeing. Indigenous conceptualisations of socio-emotional wellbeing emphasise the importance of social support derived from feelings of interconnectedness with others and other important elements in the environment, such as connections to country or spirituality and other cultural and social relations that contribute to understandings of self.[171]

If support staff think of resilience as both a *personal state of being resilient* that fluctuates in response to the challenges that students confront and *a process* through which resilience develops over time while overcoming or coping with adversities, then *mediating factors* are of paramount importance to students' capacities to bounce back or cope. Student support is a major mediating factor for developing Indigenous students' resilience in the face of setbacks and adversity during their studies. For example, the first two of the three students quoted below[172] had benefited from advice from support staff about dealing with disappointment in their learning efforts, which provided alternative ways of understanding their situations and more positive ways to self-message; the third had developed her own strategy:

> I think [my resilience has improved] … Last year where I got a bad mark or something, I would just beat my head and be like, 'Oh I can't do this, why am I even at uni,' … whereas now, well you do get upset, you get down, but you just use that to improve.

> You are bound to have your occasional missteps, and that's ok as long as you take something away from that is what matters. In those sorts of circumstances where you might feel a bit disappointed with yourself, it's not the mark that matters the most; it's the feedback that matters and how you can improve.

> I always have to tell myself when I'm going badly, well, first, compared to who and, second, it's meant to be difficult, it's designed that way, which I think a lot of students don't really understand.

From our research with students and through the experiences of working with support staff, we know that in the face of minor setbacks that are either personal or related to learning, some students have sufficient inner resources or supportive social networks to be resilient and some do not. These students will need assistance to keep their spirits and self-belief up when they experience a setback. However, even resilient students sometimes do not have sufficient inner resources or support networks to deal with constant or multiple and intersecting setbacks or a major adverse event, such as a death in the family or other major life disruption. Students experiencing major setbacks require sound practical advice about managing any prolonged absence from study and strategies to manage emotionally. Students who do not bounce back from learning setbacks or more minor setbacks in their lives or encounter chronic forms of adversity are at risk of becoming disheartened, demotivated, and depressed and of withdrawing from studies. Support staff must be aware of students who face both acute and chronic adversity by being familiar with their circumstances, their academic progress, and the extent and helpfulness of their supportive social networks, and by reviewing how they are at appropriate points in time. Support staff also need to be mindful of students who do not have supportive social networks, especially those who are away from home for the first time or have had major disruptions to their established support networks.

For understanding and serving all Indigenous students, it is helpful to remember that the literature also suggests that *resistance* is sometimes deployed as a source of resilience. Being resilient in the face of setbacks often requires acceptance, adjustment, or a change of perspective by individuals, which can produce tensions concerning notions of survival and 'acceptance of the prevailing order.'[173] For some Indigenous students, withdrawal from university studies is a form of resistance to the dominance of the prevailing order, which marginalises Indigenous people's presence, concerns, and historical and contemporary experiences and knowledge. Students who have difficulties with the link between resilience and adjustment, acceptance or transformation can be assisted by developing an understanding of adaptation as Indigenous continuity amid change. That is, setbacks that produce reactions of resistance can be used to turn resistance into perseverance to develop the knowledge and skills to contest prevailing knowledge and discourses, and to continue developing and drawing on their Indigenous perspectives.[174] This may provide such students with an alternative option to withdrawing from higher education studies.

Nevertheless, it needs to be remembered that for some Indigenous students, the capacity to keep generating their inner reserves of resilience can be exhausting in the face of chronic adversity. This is especially the case in the face of their knowledge of the continuing systemic production of Indigenous social and economic adversity and knowledge production that appears to do little to disrupt the prevailing sets of understandings about Indigenous people. The students' wellbeing must be at the forefront for support staff working to support them in these sorts of situations.

A major critique of the resilience discourse (i.e., how it is talked about in the context of its use, value, and benefits for individuals to overcome adversity) is its convenient 'ideological fit' with neoliberal discourses that shift responsibilities for the life circumstances in which vulnerable people find themselves onto individuals and away from the responsibilities of the State to its citizens.[175]

Despite this criticism, there are increased references to resilience in health and wellbeing policy program contexts in the higher education context. Resilience has been conceptualised as a bridge between education and mental health, and resilience education for university students has gained some acceptance.[176]

Transition

Transition is a key concept in higher education. Student transitions in higher education are of interest to universities because of concerns about student attrition and outcomes. Universities' efforts to ease and manage student transitions are considered an important enabler of student retention, persistence, engagement, and belonging.[177]

The research literature reveals different ways of understanding transitions, some of which we think will resonate with the Indigenous student support sector and be useful considerations for understanding students' challenges and efforts to manage these challenges. The literature on higher education transitions is a subset of the higher education literature and the wider literature on life transitions, which crosses a range of disciplines, such as sociology, psychology, and social work. There are no settled definitions of what constitutes a transition. Two useful positions on transition proposed in the higher education sector are 'change navigated by students in their movement within and through formal education'[178] and 'the capability to navigate change.'[179]

Discussions in the literature about how universities can support student transitions conceptualise transition in a range of ways. Transition is commonly conceptualised as a period of adjustment or phases of adjustment involving linear progressions of students in which they align their adjustments to institutional expectations. This understanding considers transition in terms of bounded periods along a pathway, for example, beginning to think about university, preparing for university, familiarisation with and orientation to university cultures, first-year experiences, and adjustments during the middle and final years of university.[180] Institutional responses to ease students' adjustment focus on the first-year experience, which is considered critical for students' retention.[181] These institutional responses include induction programs, student support services, co-curricular activities, such as orientation programs and academic skills workshops, and integrated information delivery related to procedural, curricula, and assessment requirements.[182]

Another conceptualisation of transition focuses on stages of student development—the changes that occur *within individuals* through their engagement with academic learning and cultures. In this conceptualisation, transitions are still considered linear and understood as 'complex transformations made up of a series of smaller changes in aspects of individuals, such as their attitudes, values, beliefs, understanding and skills, which lead to changes in self-concept and learning.'[183] Developing students' identities to include learner identities or student/discipline identities as preparation for assuming professional/career identities aligns with this understanding. One student transitioning from theoretical learning to clinical practice described this process as follows: 'before you still felt like, "I'm just a student," and you still are a student, but you actually feel like you are involved in something and you can actually see, "this is where I'm going."'[184] While the development of students' identities is understood to proceed through stages, these are less bounded by time, with individuals' various transitions and adjustments more dependent on the complex interplay between individual, social, and institutional variables.

A further conceptualisation criticises the institutional perspectives of transition by questioning the idea of linear progressions towards a fixed destination and the idea that there is a universal experience of transition common to all students. In this line of thinking, transitions cannot be understood only through the institutional perspective of inducting students into university cultures and practices or at the level of individual change. Rather, student development is 'fundamentally situated within social contexts,'[185] and individuals 'are not situated within fixed identities or roles either before or after ... the move to higher education.'[186] For these scholars, transition is understood:

> as an almost permanent state of being and becoming. Identity is not viewed as static or as something which is eventually fully formed. Students ... may over time develop a student or learner identity, but they will also have an identity, as, for example, a parent or as an employee[187]

or, we should add, as an Indigenous Australian.

This conceptualisation of student transition has emerged in the presence of diverse groups of students and the changing context of higher education. In this conceptualisation, transitions are considered multiple, micro, and varied, a daily feature of life and negotiated on a daily basis; for example, transitions between home and university, work and university, and between different identities and 'selves,' such as parent, daughter, partner, student, employee, carer, or friend—to which we might add Indigenous/group/community identities or 'selves.' In this conceptualisation, understanding transition as a linear or staged process is considered insensitive to the actual life experiences of many students who do not enter higher education on a linear pathway from school to a career destination but whose lives move in back-and-forth and in-and-out movements as their circumstances change and they move around while meeting a range of daily obligations.[188] This suggests students are engaged in sideways or horizontal transitions and a series of upwards academic learning movements.

University approaches to easing students' transitions align mainly with the first conceptualisation above; for example, the vast array of student services in place in universities to assist students' adjustment to the university and academic expectations (e.g., pathway and preparation programs, orientation programs, first-year experience strategies, buddy/peer mentor systems, academic skills workshops, and other student support services, including Indigenous student support provisions). However, Indigenous student support services have long been sensitive to Indigenous students' various pathways into university, movements in and out of their studies, and heightened levels of cultural disorientation to higher education practices and environments that often cause difficult adjustments and transitions for some students.[189]

The three conceptualisations, which characterise student transitions either as linear, developmental, or socially contextualised, offer useful background knowledge for Indigenous student support staff. Pre-undergraduate pathways and preparation programs, orientation and induction activities, intense early transition support (before census date), and a first-year emphasis on support make sense for students who are likely to find the movement into university a stressful, anxious, or overwhelming experience. The second and third conceptualisations indicate the complexity of the student support role in easing Indigenous students' transitions. For example, the idea of transition as stages of student development and change implies that support staff must also attend to students' individual experiences to meet their needs for support in an ongoing manner. This conceptualisation also implies that support staff need some awareness of what is involved in students' transition experiences, for example, the shifts in personal beliefs, attitudes, and identities that occur through engagement in formal and informal learning situations and how this might affect their motivation, persistence, or wellbeing.

The conceptualisation of transition as a permanent state of being, characterised by the horizontal shifts between different life domains, roles, and identities, and vertical shifts in understandings of self and the world that occur through engaging with academic learning, resemble the experiences of many Indigenous students. Students who have challenges related to personal journeys or moving between their different roles and obligations, students who are unsettled by a sense of emerging shifts in their beliefs, values, or identities or the tensions between academic knowledge and their own knowledge and experiences, will not likely find adequate support through university induction, orientation, academic skills, and general information sessions. These students will require much more personalised support from Indigenous staff who understand these experiences.

In summary, these conceptualisations suggest that transitions for Indigenous students are experienced in multiple and individual ways during their studies and that structured program responses, such as induction programs, while beneficial, will need to be supplemented by individual support throughout their studies, especially when a student's higher education journey involves moving in and out of their studies as their personal circumstances permit. This might sound onerous for staff; however, the reality is that the work of supporting student transitions is the work of student support services.

Combining the concepts discussed in this section demonstrates that the capabilities required for a successful transition are those required to overcome the range of challenges that Indigenous students experience, which are also those needed for progress and success in learning. However, the conceptualisations of transition suggest it is a mistake to think that progress and success in learning delineates an endpoint in students' transition experiences. Nevertheless, different stages of the educational journey require staff to consider what aspects of transition their strategy emphasis should be focused on for students at different stages of progression and according to the complex mix of individual, social, and institutional variables that produce individual challenges. Certainly, preparation, pre-semester orientation, the first six weeks, and first-year experiences are specific periods that provide opportunities for supporting Indigenous students' adjustments to higher education demands and expectations. However, support staff must also consider the different micro-transitions that students experience on a daily basis and whether and how their capacity to manage these negatively affects their chances of academic success or their emotional wellbeing. Staff must be in contact with all their students to understand students' individual experiences and provide constructive assistance. This applies to students who have deferred studies. Keeping in contact with these students and offering assistance when they return helps with the transition movements in and out of study for Indigenous students in these circumstances.

Student health and socio-emotional wellbeing

Students' health and socio-emotional wellbeing is an area that requires thoughtful and ethical consideration as an element of the student support process. This section presents basic information and minimal research on the topic related to Indigenous people and higher education students. Any professional development or workshopping with staff on this topic should always consider recruiting those with expertise in this area.

The concept of health and wellbeing encompasses physical and mental health and wellbeing. The influences that determine an individual's health and wellbeing include a complex interplay of health behaviours, access to and use of health services, and environmental, inherited, and prior experience factors.[190] Studies and student experience surveys have shown that mental ill-health negatively influences academic outcomes, by 'impair[ing] students' learning, impacting on their attention, cognition, problem-solving, social interactions and the capacity to work constructively with others or to engage effectively with learning activities.'[191] In contrast, positive mental wellbeing 'means students will have the resilience, motivation and persistence needed to engage effectively in complex learning tasks, manage stressors, respond positively to challenges and make the most of the opportunities available.'[192]

From the medical perspective, mental health is an umbrella term covering a spectrum from mental ill-health and medically diagnosable disorders to mental wellbeing and flourishing. Mental health is 'a state of well-being in which the individual realizes [sic] his or her own abilities, can cope with the normal stresses of life, can work productively and fruitfully, and is able to make a contribution to his or her community.'[193] A person with a medically diagnosed mental illness or disorder, such as bipolar or an anxiety disorder, can achieve a state of wellbeing if effectively treated. Conversely, a person who generally experiences a sense of wellbeing can experience mental difficulties in response to numerous factors, such as life pressures, environmental factors, and changes in physical health.[194]

However, from the Indigenous perspective:

> Aboriginal health is not just the physical well-being of an individual but refers to the social, emotional and cultural well-being of the whole Community in which each individual is able to achieve their full potential as a human being, thereby bringing about the total well-being of their Community. It is a whole of life view and includes the cyclical concept of life-death-life.[195]

Indigenous Australians tend to stress *socio-emotional wellbeing* rather than mental illness or difficulties:

> Many Aboriginal and Torres Strait Islander people believe that mental health and mental illness focus too much on problems and don't properly describe all the factors that make up and influence wellbeing. Because of this, most Aboriginal and Torres Strait Islander people prefer the term social and emotional wellbeing as it fits well with a holistic view of health.[196]

The emphasis on influences on socio-emotional wellbeing also reflects that the disparities between Indigenous Australians' health and wellbeing and those of non-Indigenous Australians are linked to the underlying social determinants of Indigenous health, which are known to affect Indigenous people's overall health and wellbeing significantly.[197] Social determinants are 'the circumstances in which people grow, live, work and age.'[198] A recent review of relevant Indigenous literature[199] identified the following nine specific Indigenous domains of wellbeing: autonomy, empowerment, and recognition; family and community; culture, spirituality, and identity; country; basic needs; work, roles, and responsibilities; education; physical health; and mental health. Most of the literature reviewed emphasised the connectedness and interplay between and within these domains and the importance of *connectedness* for socio-emotional wellbeing.

These Indigenous domains of wellbeing reflect the sociocultural knowledge and understandings of Indigenous societies. However, they also highlight the devastation of Indigenous Australians' political, economic, and social structures by colonisation and government policies, continuing failure of remedies to address ongoing disadvantages, effects of racism and discrimination, and continuing effects of this legacy on Indigenous people's health and wellbeing. For other Australians, social determinants generally include an individual's income, education, employment, and social support and inclusion, which also include such things as access to and use of information and services, green spaces, playgrounds, housing, and other factors associated with levels of income, education, and employment.[200]

Students' mental wellbeing is a significant part of all students' wellbeing and an increasing concern of universities.[201] One in four young people aged between 15 and 24 will experience mental ill-health in any one year. Three in five of these young people are university students.[202] A 2009 study of Indigenous students across eight universities found that 37% of students interviewed reported a mental health disorder or a family member with one.[203] Although universities are now increasing their attention in this area, there is no regular data collection or monitoring of university students' mental wellbeing and not much research relating to the higher education context.[204]

Studies have identified various risk factors contributing to mental ill-health among university students, including under-preparedness, academic pressures, financial pressures, challenges associated with relocation and transitions, social isolation, drug and alcohol use, poor physical health, poor diets, a lack of sleep, and controlling parental expectations.[205] Although students' difficulties in some areas were associated with a lack of independent living skills, financial pressures and employment hours also contributed to students' levels of psychological distress.[206]

Mental health difficulties, associated with psychological distress, can be experienced at any time.[207] At lower levels, stress can be motivating and productive. However, when moods, anxiety, and stress are severe or prolonged, they can cause high levels of psychological distress, which can cause 'diminished attention, memory, planning, decision-making, impulse control and information processing capacities—all of which negatively impact learning.'[208] The pressure associated with study can also make it difficult for students with diagnosed mental disorders to manage with their usual strategies.[209]

Apart from international students, in Australian universities, the following groups have been identified as being at risk of mental difficulties: law and medicine students, rural and regional students (to which we need to add remote area students), students from low socio-economic backgrounds, Aboriginal and Torres Strait Islander students, and students with physical disabilities.[210] The transition period is understood to be a risk period for commencing students, especially young students who are still transitioning from adolescence to adulthood and often learning to self-manage and balance various life demands for the first time.[211]

Universities are increasing their awareness of the importance of students' access to services, opportunities for knowledge and skills development and providing supportive environments, responsive teaching and curricula, and services in the mental wellbeing area to assist students' mental health and wellbeing.[212] A large part of the Indigenous student support pastoral role focuses on assisting distressed students who are experiencing difficulties. However, there appears to be a complex interplay between many factors—academic and environmental (university and external)—and students' own levels of inner resources and skills for managing socio-emotional aspects of learning and events in their lives.

There are some essential supports that assist students' socio-emotional wellbeing at university. The University of Melbourne's Enhancing Student Wellbeing strategy outlines five essentials that students require:

- autonomous motivation
- a sense of belonging
- positive relationships
- experiences of autonomy
- feelings of competence.[213]

These draw attention to the importance of students' access to social and learning support. These also draw attention to the role that teaching academics and curricula can play in the development of students' resilience and mental health, in addition to providing students access to mental health information and services.

The more useful and practical details of these essentials are closely related to many of the discussions of concepts included so far in this chapter. These include:

- developing a sense of belonging and connectedness to others and environments that are inclusive and promote respectful interactions and relationships
- understanding diverse students' needs and the importance of supporting their learning
- teaching engagements that foster students' intrinsic interests, communicate the value of knowledge and skills, build students' self-efficacy, offer choice and flexibility, and create social connections between students and academics
- providing opportunities for students to develop time and task management, reflection and self-understanding, self-regulation, goal setting, and help-seeking
- understanding the value of assisting students to develop self-management skills and resilience for wellbeing and employability
- facilitating access to appropriate services for health counselling and academic considerations.[214]

Most of these reflect what student support staff should already be doing as part of their role in assisting students to manage difficult situations that cause distress more effectively before they become debilitating and threaten their health and studies.

Students' episodes of physical illnesses or chronic illnesses can also affect learning outcomes and mental wellbeing. Students experiencing physical and socio-emotional wellbeing issues will likely need assistance navigating university rules and processes to reduce the possible negative effects. It is also important to remember that students with a classified disability are understood to be at risk of experiencing threats to their socio-emotional wellbeing and are likely to need assistance with navigating special provisions and accessing appropriate services.

One of the most challenging aspects of assisting students experiencing high levels of distress is the reluctance of many students to ask for help. This suggests that support staff need to be in regular contact with students and have developed trusting relationships that give students the confidence to come forward when experiencing levels of anxiety, stress, and distress or illness that are difficult to discuss, or that they cannot manage on their own or are affecting their studies. It may also be helpful for support staff to be aware of the differences between short-term academic stress associated with deadlines, long-term stresses associated with transitioning into a more independent life, particularly for those living away from home for the first time and those without sufficient networks of social support, and the effects on wellbeing and achievement for those with short-term or chronic personal difficulties.

Student finance, accommodation, employment, and commute times

This section highlights some key study conditions that significantly influence Indigenous students' capacities to participate and stay in their studies, their chances of achieving successful outcomes, and their socio-emotional wellbeing. These are issues that are very familiar to all who are involved in Indigenous higher education today.

Almost all reports on Indigenous higher education identify finance as a major barrier for Indigenous students.[215] Compared to other students, Indigenous students are more likely to:

- be older with dependents to support
- go without food and basic necessities while in study
- worry about or not feel in control of their finances
- miss classes because of employment commitments
- be more likely to defer or reduce their course loads because of inadequate finance.

As well, a greater percentage of Indigenous students rely on student income support.[216]

Adequate finance is essential for optimal or at least favourable study conditions, and favourable study conditions enable academic achievement. Securing favourable study conditions requires a stable and sufficient income source. Financial uncertainty is unsettling and a source of anxiety for many Indigenous students. Financial worries affect students' health and wellbeing and negatively affect academic success. There are seemingly endless difficulties associated with meeting the criteria for government financial assistance and accessing it in time to be ready for the commencement of a semester.

Many scholarships available in universities are only for students who qualify for government assistance. The continuation of many scholarships is often conditional on students' passing all their subjects or maintaining a specific grade point average (GPA), often a credit average. Whatever their eligibility criteria, the vast majority of scholarships do not meet the costs of studying, although they provide an important source of supplementary income for students. There are, of course, some very generous scholarships awarded on a merit basis. The eligibility criteria and reporting requirements in the government's funding support programs (e.g., ABSTUDY) militate against the concerted efforts mounted each year to improve national education priority areas in the 'Closing the Gap' agenda. As Indigenous pastoral support staff know from experience of assisting students with financial issues, the intersections between incomes earned through scholarships, part-time and casual employment, particularly fluctuating incomes, and regulations concerning entitlements to government financial assistance cause endless problems and worries for students who mostly survive from week to week.

Apart from the anxiety and the tax on personal wellbeing that insufficient or uncertain finance imposes on students, employment commitments mean that underprepared students who require extra time and effort to succeed have less time than they need for studying. Many Indigenous students are forced to reduce their subject loads or go in and out of their studies as finance permits. This extends their years of study and either risks their full-time status and, thus, their financial assistance, or reduces them to part-time status, which extends their study for a longer period.

Stable and suitable accommodation is also essential for favourable study conditions and overlaps with finance issues. The costs of relocation for regional students and accommodation on campus or around universities in metropolitan areas force many students into unsatisfactory arrangements or long daily commutes. While some scholarship foundations and residential colleges on campuses provide increased places and generous residential scholarships for Indigenous students, they are not a suitable option for all Indigenous students and generally only cover teaching and exam periods.[217] In metropolitan areas, private accommodation close to universities is mostly prohibitively expensive for many Indigenous students. As a result, many Indigenous students have long daily commutes to and from university.

Understanding students' personal situations and providing assistance in these areas—finance, accommodation, employment, and travel times—are a large part of the pastoral support role. While Indigenous student support staff generally understand students' difficulties with finances, accommodation, travel times, employment commitments, and carer obligations and are practised at assisting students, there can be tensions regarding the lines between student and staff responsibilities in these areas. Similar to supporting students to take control of their learning, pastoral support should help students develop the confidence and skills to resolve difficulties in these areas. This suggests supporting students to determine and practise how to do things for themselves. For example, modelling or rehearsing how to interact with Centrelink or the scholarships office develops students' confidence to manage independently. Likewise, guiding form-filling, which can be daunting for young students with little experience, explaining regulations, rules, and procedures, distributing scholarship information promptly so that students have sufficient time to apply effectively, assisting them with the application process and proofreading forms and applications so that students include all requested information or learn what they need to emphasise can increase their chances of gaining a scholarship or job.

Finance, accommodation, employment, and travel issues are also major areas for assistance from senior university staff, student support managers and staff. For staff, this entails:

- establishing good relationships with Centrelink staff
- arranging for Indigenous Centrelink staff to visit the university to provide information and resolve student issues at the beginning of each semester (this helps personalise the Centrelink experience for anxious or frustrated students)
- establishing good relationships with university scholarships offices so that they become aware of student issues and support staff can help ensure students respond to scholarship office requirements
- sourcing and maintaining updated lists of suitable scholarships for students and becoming familiar with scholarships' levels of finance, eligibility criteria, conditions, application deadlines, payment disbursement details, and requirements to report student progress
- distributing scholarship information promptly so applications are not rushed
- collecting sources of student employment and dispersing information to students having difficulty finding suitable employment (this includes establishing relations with other sections of the university who offer casual work to students)
- establishing good relations with residential colleges and university accommodation officers to improve Indigenous students' access to accommodation
- including finance, accommodation, and travel situations in students' profile records and updating changes in students' circumstances (i.e., monitoring to ensure students are not facing challenges in these areas that could threaten their chances of success or wellbeing).

Managers and senior university staff, if necessary or appropriate, can assist behind the scenes with managers of other sections of the university and other relevant agencies by making a case for working together, securing timely information distribution, workable processes, or assistance for students. Cooperation and agreement at a higher level enable support staff efforts and protect against the loss of relationships when individual staff members leave. Decisions about who is responsible for soliciting sources of financial assistance, such as scholarships, depend to some extent on each university's particular arrangements. While student support managers should be able to source available avenues of finance for students, senior university staff are more weighty advocates for finding new sources of finance and are perhaps best placed to interact with corporate and private scholarship donors, university foundations, residential colleges, or the scholarship offices of smaller universities.

Sourcing more avenues of financial assistance for Indigenous students requires a high level of relationship building and cooperation between all the parties involved. Donors often have their own ideas and can sometimes lack awareness of Indigenous students' particular challenges and what is needed for them to succeed. One area that can require negotiation with donors is the expectation that students will regularly attend workplaces or functions or make speeches. These provide excellent opportunities for students to build relationships and networks, gain knowledge, and develop their public speaking and social skills. Some students gain great benefits from these opportunities; others find these expectations very stressful. In some cases, tactful interventions on behalf of students may be required.

These expectations sometimes extend to Indigenous employment services. Although there are mostly great benefits for students that should not be underestimated, not all students aspire to public or leadership roles but, rather, aspire to be good professionals—teachers, doctors, nurses, allied health workers, or social workers—who want to work in their own communities. Some wonderful donors build relationships with the students they are assisting financially by taking an interest in them, their academic progress, their general happiness, and their future employment, without applying pressure to 'perform' for others. This is an excellent donor strategy for shy or socially unconfident students because it widens their social experiences and provides donors with information that might lead to them activating their own networks on behalf of their students' future prospects. We know of donors who have kept faith in their scholarship recipients through deferment periods and changes of courses and encouraged them through supportive contact and advice through to graduation. However, sometimes, it is necessary to discuss with some donors what their expectations of students are. These discussions are perhaps the realm of the senior university staff, with input and feedback from managers and staff about the particular pressures students sometimes encounter in these situations.

Care must also be taken that extracurricular demands placed on scholarship recipients by donors do not take too much time away from students' study requirements or clash with students' schedules, especially assessment schedules. Donors want the best for the students they support and are generous in their inclusion of students in extracurricular activities; however, they are not always aware of the pressures students experience. Some donors choose not to interact with their recipients, and this choice needs to be respected. Nevertheless, it is a good strategy to have scholarship recipients acknowledge the generosity of their donors by sending a thank you note on receipt of a scholarship and at the end of their studies, in addition to any required reporting of student progress.

Implications for student support

The concepts and study conditions discussed throughout Chapter 1 are key to Indigenous students' higher education outcomes. They provide important insights into what is involved or relevant to the student effort to succeed. This section provides three main points about the implications for improving Indigenous student support efforts.

Timely, individualised support for all Indigenous students

Because the majority of Indigenous students are underprepared for higher education study and/or university life and because there is such a complex interplay between the various individual, institutional, and external factors that can positively or negatively influence a student's outcomes, support staff cannot escape the implication that Indigenous students need individualised support. Although current Indigenous student support practices across the nation primarily attend to individual student needs, the task of lifting Indigenous students' rates of success, progress, and completion suggests that attending to *all* Indigenous students' individual needs for support is required. This includes more than just those students who ask for help on their own initiative, have failed subjects, are at risk of exclusion, or come to the attention of Indigenous support staff through referrals from elsewhere in the university.

Lifting overall student outcomes implies meeting all Indigenous students' needs for support. Because the various influences on student success affect individual students differently and at different times, the implication is that staff should know all their students and how they are managing over time to understand which students need assistance for specific challenges at certain points in time. Further, because student's experiences of success influence their beliefs in their own abilities, sense of their competency, motivation levels, emotions, approach to future tasks, willingness to persist through challenges, sense of belonging, and quality of engagement, the implication is that support for students needs to be provided *in time* and in ways that help them experience incremental successes and improvements in minor and major academic tasks and eventually take control with minimal support.

Implementing support strategies to help students develop the capabilities for managing academic learning and personal challenges

The research work presented throughout this chapter has highlighted that students require support to manage challenges associated with their academic learning, personal issues, challenging life events, obligations, and study conditions to succeed. Students need to develop their existing repertoire of cognitive, metacognitive, affective, and motivational skills to manage these challenges. In less academic terms, these refer to students' higher-order mental processing skills, strategic skills for managing how they function in their learning tasks, their ability to manage emotions that negatively influence their outcomes, and their willingness to apply these skills when approaching their academic learning tasks.

Research knowledge regarding the role of emotions, belonging, resilience, and socio-emotional wellbeing in academic learning success confirms the critical role of social and cultural support provided by pastoral support staff. However, the influence of students' personal attributes, challenges, and emotional skill levels on academic learning and the influence of academic learning challenges on students' socio-emotional wellbeing implies the need for clarity regarding student support roles. We suggest there is a case for managers to be more mindful of how academic support, pastoral support, and supplementary tutor roles function together to assist students. Simultaneously, closer cooperation between academic and pastoral support roles to support students more effectively needs to be mindful of the importance of the distinct academic and pastoral skill sets required for these roles. We strongly believe that relying on supplementary tutors alone for academic support is insufficient to support students effectively and that dedicated academic support officers should complement pastoral support teams.

Efficient systems for monitoring, managing, and utilising student progress data and outcomes and the effectiveness of support strategies

The need for individualised and well-coordinated academic and personal support implies the need for efficient systems for support staff to monitor and track student progress and keep abreast of students' learning issues and needs in time to prevent student failures. Monitoring systems also need to monitor and track any changes in student circumstances, such as finances, accommodation, employment, or other obligations, that may negatively affect their emotional wellbeing, academic outcomes, or ability to continue with their studies. Likewise, the development of individual students' capacities to eventually manage independently with minimal support implies a process for assessing, measuring, and documenting students' movements towards greater independence in learning regarding the key influences on student success in academia, study conditions, and socio-emotional wellbeing. The role of staff in developing individual students' capabilities also implies they need to keep track of the academic and pastoral interventions and strategies they have suggested/applied to individual students to follow up and gauge their effectiveness, including the effectiveness of supplementary tutorial support. Finally, students' progress should, ideally, be reported in a way that provides sufficient feedback for staff to review and adjust their strategies and practices when student outcomes indicate areas for improvement.

Notes

1   First-year enabling student. Unless otherwise cited, all student quotations in this document are from interviewees in the persistence study.
2   For examples, see Kift & Field, 2009.
3   See Broad, 2006; McKendry & Boyd, 2012.
4   Balapumi & Aitken, 2012, p. 2.
5   Holec, 1979, p. 3, as cited in Broad, 2006, p. 120.
6   See Zimmermann, 2002; Lau, 2017.
7   See the following sections in this chapter: 'Self-regulation'; 'Motivation and persistence'; 'Resilience.'
8   Zimmerman et al., 1996.
9   Zimmermann, 2002, p. 65.
10   Schuster et al., 2020.
11   McCombs & Marzano, 1990; Meyer, 2010.
12   Second-year student.
13   First-year enabling student.
14   Fourth-year student.
15   See the section on self-regulation in this chapter.
16   See Field et al., 2014.
17   Conley, 2007, p. 1, as cited in Lemmens, 2011, p. 26.
18   Kift, 2009.
19   Lemmens, 2011.
20   Lipman, 2015.
21   See Lipman, 2015.

22 See the following sections in this chapter: 'Self-efficacy and academic self-efficacy'; 'Self-regulation,' for more detail.
23 See, e.g., McCombs & Marzano, 1990; Robbins et al., 2004; Lipman, 2015.
24 See, e.g., Behrendt et al., 2012; Kinnane et al., 2014.
25 See, e.g., Barney, 2016; Bourke et al., 1996; Oliver et al., 2013a, 2013b, 2016; Page et al., 1997; Schwartz, 2018; Taylor et al., 2019.
26 See Pekrun et al., 2002.
27 For insights into how supplementary tutors assist students, see Nakata et al., 2019b.
28 Bandura, 2006, p. 164.
29 Bandura, 2006.
30 Bandura, 2006.
31 Bandura, 2009a, p. 8.
32 Bandura, 2006, p. 170.
33 Bandura, 2009b; Pajares, 1996.
34 Bandura & Locke, 2003, p. 87.
35 Bandura, 2009b, p. 179.
36 Linnenbrink & Pintrich, 2002; see also Robbins et al., 2004.
37 Bandura, 1998, p. 71.
38 Linnenbrink & Pintrich, 2002.
39 Linnenbrink & Pintrich, 2002.
40 Linnenbrink & Pintrich, 2002.
41 Second-year student.
42 Bandura, 1998.
43 First-year student.
44 Bandura, 1998.
45 For transition pedagogy, see Kift, 2009.
46 See, Nakata et al., 2019b.
47 Linnenbrink & Pintrich, 2002.
48 Second-year student.
49 First-year student who started in an enabling program.
50 Second-year student.
51 Bandura & Locke, 2003, p. 87.
52 Pintrich, 2000, p. 453, as cited in Schunk, 2005, p. 85.
53 Zimmermann, 2002, p. 65.
54 Dresel et al., 2015; Roth et al., 2016.
55 Reeves & Stich, 2011; Puustinen & Pulkkinen, 2001; Zimmermann, 2002.
56 Krause, 2005a, p. 60.
57 Cassidy, 2011; Schunk, 2005.
58 Fifth-year student who initially struggled to achieve.
59 For discussions of models, see Puustinen & Pulkkinen, 2001; Roth et al., 2016.
60 See the section in this chapter on 'Independent learning and independent learners' for more detail on this skill.
61 See, e.g., Dresel et al., 2015; McCombs & Marzano, 1990; Pekrun ct al., 2002; Puustinen & Pulkkinen, 2001; Paris & Winograd, 2003; Trigwell et al., 2012; Zimmerman, 1990.
62 We use Zimmermann (2002) and borrow from and expand on Dresel et al. (2015, p. 455) to provide a plain language description of the subtasks students might focus on in these three phases. Dresel et al. (2015) re-named Zimmermann's (2002) phases as: pre-action, action, and post-action.
63 See, e.g., Dresel et al., 2015; Roth et al., 2016.
64 McCombs & Marzano, 1990.
65 Zimmermann, 2002, pp. 69–70.
66 Zimmermann, 2002.
67 Third-year student.
68 Third-year student with performance anxiety.

69   Second-year student.
70   Jardine & Krause, 2005, p. 5.
71   Jardine & Krause, 2005, p. 5.
72   See, e.g., Bean & Metzner, 1985; Burden et al., 1998; Burrus et al., 2013; Leveson et al., 2013; Hearn et al., 2019; Jardine & Krause 2005; Kutieleh et al., 2004; Martin et al., 2017; Reason, 2009; Russell & Jarvis, 2019; Terenzini & Pascarella, 1991; Tinto, 2005.
73   See, e.g., Demetriou & Schmitz-Sciborski, 2011; Kuh et al., 2006; Pascarella & Terenzini, 2005; Reason, 2009; Robbins et al., 2004; Terenzini & Pascarella, 1991; Tinto, 1975. For Indigenous and Australian student experience studies, see, e.g., Barney, 2016; Krause, 2005a; Leveson et al., 2013; Oliver et al., 2016; Rigney & Neill, 2018. See also the Student Experience Survey by Quality Indicators for Learning and Teaching (https://www.qilt.edu.au/qilt-surveys/student-experience) and the Australian Survey of Student Experiences (AUSSE) website (https://www.acer.org/au/ausse).
74   See, e.g., Braxton et al., 2014; Demetriou et al., 2011; Kuh et al., 2006; Pascarella & Terenzini, 2005; Reason, 2009; Robbins et al., 2004; Tinto, 1975, 2005, 2015.
75   See, e.g., reports of Student Experience Surveys from Quality Indicators for Teaching and Learning, at https://www.qilt.edu.au/surveys/student-experience-survey-(ses).
76   See, e.g., Barney, 2016; Rigney & Neill, 2018; and other Indigenous student experience studies.
77   Eccles & Wigfield, 2002; Graham & Weiner, 1996.
78   See, e.g., Covington, 2000; Graham & Weiner, 1996; McCombs & Marzano, 1990; Pekrun et al., 2002.
79   See, e.g., Linnenbrink & Pintrich, 2002; Ryan & Deci, 2000b.
80   Second-year student.
81   Second-year student.
82   First-year student.
83   Second-year student.
84   First-year student.
85   Second-year student.
86   See, e.g., Bandura, 1998; Covington, 2000; Ryan & Deci, 2000b.
87   For an overview of motivation theories, constructs and studies, see Covington, 2000; Eccles & Wigfield, 2002; Graham & Weiner, 1996.
88   See, e.g., references in this section.
89   See Covington, 2000; Schunk, 1990.
90   Schunk, 1990.
91   See Eccles & Wigfield 2002.
92   Eccles & Wigfield, 2002.
93   Pajares, 1996.
94   See Graham & Weiner, 1996; Eccles & Wigfield, 2002.
95   Schunk & Zimmerman, 2006, as cited in Demetriou & Schmitz-Sciborski, 2011, p. 6.
96   See Demetriou & Schmitz-Sciborski, 2011.
97   See Ryan & Deci, 2000a, 2000b.
98   See Ryan & Deci, 2000a, 2000b.
99   Ryan & Deci, 2000a, p. 58.
100   Ryan & Deci, 2000a, p. 58.
101   See, e.g., Krause & Armitage, 2014; Thomas, 2012; Zepke, 2013, 2014.
102   See, Trowler, 2010, for a review of the scope of the student engagement literature.
103   Coates, 2008, p. vi, as cited in Krause & Armitage, 2014, p. 3.
104   Krause & Coates, 2008, p. 494.
105   McInnes, 2003, p. 9.
106   See, e.g., Kahu, 2013; Krause, 2011; Krause & Armitage, 2014; Kuh, 2009; Kuh et al., 2006; Nelson et al., 2012; Pascarella & Terenzini, 2005; Trowler, 2010; Zepke, 2013, 2014; Zepke et al., 2010a, 2010b. See also, AUSSE, the Australasian surveys of student engagement, available at https://www.acer.org/au/ausse/report.

107 Krause & Armitage, 2014, p. 3.
108 See, e.g., Kahu, 2013; Zepke et al., 2012.
109 Krause & Coates, 2008.
110 See Axelson & Flick, 2010; Zepke, 2014.
111 Trowler, 2010.
112 Trowler & Trowler, 2010, p. 9.
113 Trowler & Trowler, 2010, pp. 8–9.
114 Analysis involves thoroughly examining authors' propositions and arguments by breaking them down. Synthesis involves combining ideas from a range of sources to map common ideas or arguments. Evaluation involves students' assessments of authors' claims and arguments.
115 Zepke et al., 2012.
116 Trowler & Trowler, 2010, p. 12.
117 Trowler & Trowler, 2010, p. 12.
118 Krause, 2005b; Trowler 2010; Trowler & Trowler, 2010.
119 See, Trowler & Trowler, 2010, p. 13.
120 AUSSE & ACER, 2009.
121 Asmar et al., 2011.
122 Burke et al., 2016, p. 50.
123 See Trowler & Trowler, 2010.
124 Third-year student.
125 Many of these needs have come from interviewees (students) and support staff; many students admitted that they could be more organised.
126 See, e.g., Ahn & Davis, 2020; Carter et al., 2018; Masika & Jones, 2016; Thomas, 2012; Tinto, 2012.
127 Ahn & Davis, 2020; Thomas, 2012.
128 Second-year student.
129 Second- and first-year students, respectively.
130 Thomas, 2012.
131 See Tinto, 2015, p. 5.
132 Burke et al., 2016.
133 See, e.g., Tinto, 1975, 2005, 2012, 2015, 2019.
134 See, e.g., Burke et al., 2016; Ahn & Davis, 2020; Masika & Jones, 2016; Read et al., 2003; Russell & Jarvis, 2019; Thomas, 2012.
135 Ahn & Davis, 2020.
136 Tinto, 2015, p. 8.
137 First-year medical student.
138 See, e.g., Ahn & Davis, 2020; Burke et al., 2016.
139 Burke et al., 2016, p. 19.
140 Burke et al., 2016, p. 33.
141 Burke et al., 2016, p. 33.
142 See Burke et al., 2016.
143 Burke et al., 2016.
144 Burke et al., 2016.
145 Fifth-year student.
146 Fifth-year student.
147 Daniels & Brooker, 2014.
148 Burke et al., 2016.
149 See, e.g., Schwartz, 2018.
150 First-year student.
151 See, e.g., Kinnane et al., 2014; Nakata et al., 2008; Rigney & Neill, 2018. For the latter point, see Asmar et al., 2011.
152 See, e.g., Barney, 2016; Pechenkina, 2019.
153 See also the section 'Indigenous knowledge and perspectives in academic learning' in this chapter for more discussion.

154 Fourth-year student.
155 See, e.g., Zepke et al., 2006.
156 Second-year student.
157 See, e.g., Burden et al., 1998; Rigney & Neill, 2018; Schwartz, 2018; Walker, 2000.
158 Nakata et al., 2008.
159 See Nakata, 2007; Nakata et al., 2008.
160 Second-year student.
161 See, e.g., Asmar et al., 2011.
162 Masters by research student.
163 Fourth-year student.
164 First-year student.
165 See van Breda, 2018.
166 van Breda, 2018.
167 Humbert & Joseph, 2019.
168 See van Breda, 2018.
169 van Breda, 2018, p. 8.
170 Van Breda, 2018.
171 See, e.g., Bond et al., 2012; Clark et al., 1999; Fleet et al., 2007; Kirmayer et al., 2011.
172 All second-year students.
173 See Humbert & Joseph, 2019, p. 218.
174 Humbert & Joseph, 2019; Nakata et al., 2008.
175 See Humbert & Joseph, 2019, p. 216; van Breda, 2018.
176 Orygen, 2017.
177 Behrendt et al., 2012; Fredericks et al., 2015; Kinnane et al., 2014.
178 Gale & Parker, 2014a, p. 734.
179 Gale & Parker, 2014a, p. 737.
180 Burnett, 2007, p. 24, as cited in Gale & Parker, 2014a, p. 739.
181 Kinnane et al., 2014.
182 Gale & Parker, 2014a, 2014b; see Kift & Field, 2009.
183 O'Donnell et al., 2016, p. 7.
184 Fourth-year student.
185 O'Donnell et al., 2016, p. 8.
186 Gale & Parker, 2014a, p. 744.
187 O'Donnell et al., 2016, p. 8.
188 Gale & Parker, 2014a, 2014b; O'Donnell et al., 2016.
189 For Indigenous references to transition, see Frawley et al., 2017; Fredericks et al., 2015; Kinnane et al., 2014; Oliver et al., 2013a.
190 See Australian Institute of Health and Welfare, 2018.
191 Orygen, 2017; Baik et al., 2017, p. 3.
192 Baik et al., 2017, p. 3.
193 See The University of Sydney, 2019.
194 See The University of Sydney, 2019.
195 Aboriginal Community Controlled Health Organisations, (n.d.).
196 Australian Indigenous Health*Info*Net, 2018.
197 Dudgeon et al., 2014.
198 See Australian Institute of Health and Welfare, 2018.
199 Butler et al., 2019.
200 Australian Indigenous HealthInfoNet, 2018.
201 See, e.g., Orygen 2017; Healthy Sydney University (n.d.); The University of Melbourne, 2016; Enhancing student wellbeing, https://unistudentwellbeing.edu.au/.
202 See Orygen, 2017.
203 See Toombs & Gorman, 2011.
204 See Orygen, The National Centre of Excellence in Youth Mental Health (Orygen), 2017.
205 See Orygen, 2017, p. 13; also see Baik et al., 2017.
206 See Orygen, 2017, p. 13.

207 Enhancing Student Wellbeing, (n.d.).
208 Stallman, 2010.
209 See University of Sydney, 2020.
210 See Orygen, 2017, p. 14.
211 See Orygen, 2017, pp. 13–14.
212 See, e.g., Enhancing Student Mental Wellbeing, Learning Module 1.3.
213 See Enhancing student wellbeing, (n.d.).
214 See Enhancing student wellbeing, (n.d.). A previous iteration—the 'Learning Modules and Framework' section—of this website set out these points. The updated website covers most of these points in *Learning Module 1.3: Wellbeing essential.*
215 See, e.g., Behrendt et al., 2012; Universities Australia, 2017.
216 See Universities Australia, 2017, for statistical comparisons between Indigenous and non-Indigenous students.
217 See Behrendt et al., 2012, p. 79.

References

Aboriginal Community Controlled Health Organisations. (n.d.). *What is the definition of Aboriginal health?* National Aboriginal Community Controlled Organisations. https://www.naccho.org.au/acchos

Ahn, M. Y. & Davis, H. H. (2020). Four domains of students' sense of belonging to university. *Studies in Higher Education, 45*(3), 622–634. https://doi.org/10.1080/03075079.2018.1564902

Asmar, C., Page, S. & Radloff, A. (2011, April). *Australasian survey of student engagement research briefings: Vol. 10.* Dispelling myths: Indigenous students' engagement with university. Australian Council for Educational Research. https://research.acer.edu.au/cgi/viewcontent.cgi?article=1001&context=ausse

AUSSE & ACER. (2009). *Australasian Survey of student engagement 2009 institution report.* https://www.acer.org/files/ausse_2009_australasian_uni_ir.pdf

Australian Indigenous Health*Info*Net. (2018). *Learn: Social and emotional wellbeing.* https://healthinfonet.ecu.edu.au/learn/health-topics/social-and-emotional-wellbeing/

Australian Institute of Health and Welfare. (2018). Social determinants and Indigenous health. In *Australia's health 2018* (Australia's Health Series No. 16. AUS 221, pp. 1–4). https://www.aihw.gov.au/getmedia/4cb92d82-ce6a-44dd-bdc1-434ee7d6e849/aihw-aus-221-chapter-6-6.pdf.aspx

Axelson, R. D. & Flick, A. (2010). Defining student engagement. *Change: The Magazine of Higher Learning, 43*(1), 38–43. https://doi.org/10.1080/00091383.2011.533096

Baik, C., Larcombe, W., Brooker, A., Wynn, J., Allen, L. Brett, M., Field, R. & James, R. (2017). *Enhancing student mental wellbeing: A handbook for academic educators.* University of Melbourne.https://ddl-resources.s3.amazonaws.com/resources/MCSHE-Student-Wellbeing-Handbook-FINAL.pdf

Balapumi, R. & Aitken, A. (2012, December 3–5). *Concepts and factors influencing independent learning in IS higher education* [Conference presentation]. 23rd Australasian Conference on Information Systems, Geelong, Australia. https://dro.deakin.edu.au/eserv/DU:30049160/balapumi-conceptsandfactors-2012.pdf

Bandura, A. (1998). Self-efficacy. In H. Friedman (Ed.), *Encyclopedia of mental health* (pp. 1–15). Academic Press. (Reprinted from *Encyclopedia of human behavior*, Vol. 4, pp. 71–81, by V. S. Ramachaudran, Ed., 1994, Academic Press). https://www.uky.edu/~eushe2/Bandura/Bandura1994EHB.pdf

Bandura, A. (2006). Toward a psychology of human agency. *Perspectives on Psychological Science, 1*(2), 164–180. https://doi.org/10.1111%2Fj.1745-6916.2006.00011.x

Bandura, A. (2009a). Agency. In D. S. Carr (Ed.), *Encyclopedia of the life course and human development* (pp. 8–11). Macmillan Reference.

Bandura, A. (2009b). Cultivate self-efficacy for personal and organizational effectiveness. In E. A. Locke (Ed.), *Handbook of principles of organization behaviour* (2nd ed., pp. 179–200). Wiley. https://www.uky.edu/~eushe2/Bandura/Bandura2009Locke.pdf

Bandura, A. & Locke, E. (2003). Negative self-efficacy and goal effects revisited. *Journal of Applied Psychology, 88*(1), 87–99. https://psycnet.apa.org/doi/10.1037/0021-9010.88.1.87

Barney, K. (2016). Listening to and learning from the experiences of Aboriginal and Torres Strait Islander students to facilitate success. *Student Success, 7*(1), 1–11. https://doi.org/10.5204/ssj.v7i1.317

Bean, J. P. & Metzner, B. S. (1985). A conceptual model of nontraditional undergraduate student attrition. *Review of Educational Research, 55*(4), 485–540. https://doi.org/10.2307/1170245

Behrendt, L., Larkin, S., Griew, R. & Kelly, P. (2012, July). *Review of higher education, access and outcomes for Aboriginal and Torres Strait Islander People final report*. Australian Government. https://www.dese.gov.au/aboriginal-and-torres-strait-islander-higher-education/review-higher-education-access-and-outcomes-aboriginal-and-torres-strait-islander-people

Bond, C., Brough, M., Spurling, G. & Hayman, N. (2012). 'It had to be my choice': Indigenous smoking cessation and negotiations of risk, resistance and resilience. *Health, Risk & Society, 14*(6), 565–581. https://doi.org/10.1080/13698575.2012.701274

Bourke, C. J., Burden, J. K. & Moore, S. (1996). *Factors affecting the performance of Aboriginal and Torres Strait Islander students at Australian universities: A case study*. Australian Government Publishing Service.

Braxton, J. M., Doyle, W. R., Hartley, H. V., III, Hirschy, A. S., Jones, W. A. & McLendon, M. K. (2014). *Rethinking college student retention*. Jossey-Bass.

Broad, J. (2006). Interpretations of independent learning in further education. *Journal of Further and Higher Education, 30*(02), 119–143. https://doi.org/10.1080/03098770600617521

Burden, J., Bourke, E. A., Bourke, C. & Rigby, K. (1998). *Access, participation, transformation: A study of factors contributing to Indigenous student attrition and retention at University of Technology Sydney*. Aboriginal Research Institute, University of South Australia.

Burke, P. J., Bennett, A., Burgess, C., Gray, K. & Southgate, E. (2016). *Capability, belonging and equity in higher education: Developing inclusive approaches*. University of Newcastle. https://nova.newcastle.edu.au/vital/access/manager/Repository/uon:32939

Burrus, J., Elliot, D., Brenneman, M., Markle, R., Carney, L., Moore, G., Betancourt, A., Jackson, T., Robbins S., Kyllonen, P. & Roberts, R. D. (2013, August). *Putting and keeping students on track: Towards a comprehensive model of college persistence and goal attainment* (Research Report ETS RR–13–14). Educational Testing Service.

Butler, T. L., Anderson, K., Garvey, G., Cunningham, J., Ratcliffe, J., Tong, A., Whop, L. J., Cass, A., Dickson, M. & Howard, K. (2019). Aboriginal and Torres Strait Islander people's domains of wellbeing: A comprehensive literature review. *Social Science & Medicine, 233*, 138–157. https://doi.org/10.1016/j.socscimed.2019.06.004

Carter, J., Hollinsworth, D., Raciti, M. & Gilbey, K. (2018). Academic 'place-making': Fostering attachment, belonging and identity for Indigenous students in Australian universities. *Teaching in Higher Education, 23*(2), 243–260. https://doi.org/10.1080/13562517.2017.1379485

Clark, C., Hartnett, P., Atkinson, J. & Shochet, I. (1999). Enhancing resilience in Indigenous people: The integration of individual, family and community interventions. *Aboriginal and Islander Health Worker Journal, 23*(4), 6–10.

Covington, M. V. (2000). Goal theory, motivation, and school achievement: An integrative review. *Annual Review of Psychology, 51*, 171–200. https://doi.org/10.1146/annurev.psych.51.1.171

Daniels, J. & Brooker, J. (2014). Student identity development in higher education: Implications for graduate attributes and work-readiness. *Educational Research, 56*(1), 65–76. https://doi.org/10.1080/00131881.2013.874157

Demetriou, C. & Schmitz-Sciborski, A. (2011). Integration, motivation, strengths and optimism: Retention theories past, present and future. In R. Hayes (Ed.), *Proceedings of the 7th national symposium on student retention* (pp. 300–312). The University of Oklahoma.

Dresel, M., Schmitz, B., Schober, B., Spiel, C., Ziegler, A., Engelschalk, T., Jöstl, G., Klug, J., Roth, A., Wimmer, B. & Steuer, G. (2015). Competencies for successful self-regulated learning in higher education: Structural model and indications drawn from expert interviews. *Studies in Higher Education, 40*(3), 454–470. https://doi.org/10.1080/03075079.2015.1004236

Dudgeon, P., Milroy, H. & Walker, R. (2014). *Working together: Aboriginal and Torres Strait Islander mental health and wellbeing principles and practice.* Commonwealth of Australia. https://www.telethonkids.org.au/globalassets/media/documents/aboriginal-health/working-together-second-edition/working-together-aboriginal-and-wellbeing-2014.pdf

Eccles, J. S. & Wigfield, A. (2002). Motivational belief, values, and goals. *Annual Review of Psychology, 53*(1), 109–132. https://doi.org/10.1146/annurev.psych.53.100901.135153

Enhancing Student Wellbeing. (n.d.) *Learning Module 1.3: Wellbeing essentials.* University of Melbourne. https://unistudentwellbeing.edu.au/student-wellbeing/wellbeing-essentials/

Field, R., Duffy, J. & Huggins, A. (2014). Independent learning skills, self-determination theory and psychological well-being: Strategies for supporting the first year university experience. In T. Creagh (Ed.), *Proceedings of the 17th international first year in higher education conference* (pp. 1–10). Queensland University of Technology. https://eprints.qut.edu.au/73556/

Fleet, A., Kitson, R., Cassady, B. & Hughes, R. (2007). University-qualified Indigenous early childhood teachers: Voices of resilience. *Australian Journal of Early Childhood, 32*(3), 17–25. https://doi.org/10.1177%2F183693910703200304

Frawley, J., Larkin, S. & Smith, J. A. (Eds.). (2017). *Indigenous pathways, transitions and participation in higher education: From policy to practice.* Springer Singapore.

Fredericks, B., Mann, J., Skinner, R., CroftWarcon, P. & McFarlane, B. (2015). Enabling Indigenous education success beyond regional borders. *Journal of Economic and Social Policy, 17*(2), Article 31–34. https://eprints.qut.edu.au/91613/

Gale, T. & Parker, S. (2014a). Navigating change: A typology of student transition in higher education. *Studies in Higher Education, 39*(5), 734–753. https://doi.org/10.1080/03075079.2012.721351

Gale, T. & Parker, S. (2014b). Navigating student transition in higher education: Induction, development, becoming. In H. Brook, D. Fergie, M. Maeorg & D. Michell (Eds.), *Universities in transition: Foregrounding social contexts of knowledge in the first year experience* (pp. 13–39). University of Adelaide Press. https://doi.org/10.20851/universities-transition

Graham, S. & Weiner, B. (1996). Theories and principles of motivation. In D. C. Berliner & R. Calfee (Eds.), *Handbook of educational psychology* (pp. 63–84). Simon & Schuster Macmillan.

Healthy Sydney University. (n.d.). *A policy brief for promoting mental wellbeing in universities.* The University of Sydney. https://www.sydney.edu.au/dam/corporate/documents/about-us/values-and-visions/healthy-sydney-university-mental-wellbeing-policy-brief.pdf

Hearn, S., Benton, M., Funnell, S. & Marmolejo-Ramos, F. (2019). Investigation of the factors contributing to Indigenous students' retention and attrition rates at the University of Adelaide. *Australian Journal of Indigenous Education, 50*(1), 1–9. https://doi.org/10.1017/jie.2019.5

Humbert, C. & Joseph, J. (2019). Introduction: The politics of resilience: Problematising current approaches. *Resilience*, 7(3), 215–223. https://doi.org/10.1080/21693293.2019. 1613738

Jardine, A. & Krause, K.-L. (2005, April). *Once they arrive how do we keep them? Student persistence research and the implications for the retention of non-traditional students*. [Conference presentation]. *Enhancing Student Success: The Role of Integrated Support Services Conference*, University of Newcastle, Australia.

Kahu, E. R. (2013). Framing student engagement in higher education. *Studies in Higher Education*, 38(5), 758–773. https://doi.org/10.1080/03075079.2011.598505

Kift, S. (2009). *Articulating a transition pedagogy to scaffold and to enhance the first year student learning experience in Australian higher education: Final report for ALTC senior fellowship program*. AustralianLearning&TeachingCouncil.https://altf.org/fellowships/articulating-a-transition-pedagogy-to-scaffold-and-enhance-the-first-year-learning-experience-in-australian-higher-education/

Kift, S. & Field, R. (2009, June 29–July 1). *Intentional first year curriculum design as a means of facilitating student engagement: Some exemplars*. [Conference presentation]. 12th Pacific Rim First Year in Higher Education Conference, 'Preparing for Tomorrow Today: The First Year Experience as Foundation', Townsville, Queensland. https://eprints.qut.edu.au/30044/1/c30044.pdf

Kinnane, S., Wilks, J., Wilson, K., Hughes, T. & Thomas, S. (2014). *'Can't be what you can't see': The transition of Aboriginal and Torres Strait Islander students into higher education. Final report 2014*. The University of Notre Dame Australia. https://www.notredame.edu.au/__data/assets/pdf_file/0020/2882/SI11-2138-OLT-Final-Report-FINAL-Web.pdf

Kirmayer, L. J., Dandeneau, S., Marshall, E., Phillips, M. K. & Williamson, K. J. (2011). Rethinking resilience from Indigenous perspectives. *Canadian Journal of Psychiatry*, 56(2), 84–91. https://doi.org/10.1177%2F070674371105600203

Krause, K.-L. (2005a). Serious thoughts about dropping out in first year: Trends, patterns and implications for higher education. *Studies in Learning, Evaluation, Innovation and Development*, 2(3), 55–68. https://hdl.handle.net/10072/15410

Krause, K.-L. (2005b). *Understanding and Promoting Student Engagement in University Learning Communities*. Paper presented as keynote address: Engaged, Inert or Otherwise Occupied?: Deconstructing the 21st Century Undergraduate Student at the James Cook University Symposium 'Sharing Scholarship in Learning and Teaching: Engaging Students'. James Cook University, Townsville/Cairns, Queensland, Australia, 21–22 September. https://melbourne-cshe.unimelb.edu.au/__data/assets/pdf_file/0007/1761523/Stud_eng.pdf

Krause, K.-L. (2011). Using student survey data to shape academic priorities and approaches. In L. Stefani (Ed.), *The effectiveness of academic development* (pp. 59–72). Routledge.

Krause, K.-L. & Armitage, L. (2014). *Australian student engagement, belonging, retention and success: A synthesis of the literature*. The Higher Education Academy. https://www.aqa.ac.nz/sites/all/files/australian_student_engagement_lit_syn_2.pdf

Krause, K.-L. & Coates, H. (2008). Students' engagement in first-year university. *Assessment & Evaluation in Higher Education*, 33(5), 493–505. https://doi.org/10.1080/02602930701698892

Kuh, G. D. (2009). What student affairs professionals need to know about student engagement. *Journal of College Student Development*, 50(6), 683–704. https://doi.org/10.1353/csd.0.0099

Kuh, G. D., Kinzie, J., Buckley, J. A., Bridges, B. K. & Hayek, J. C. (2006, July). *What matters to student success: A review of the literature. Commissioned report for the national symposium on postsecondary student success: Spearheading a dialog on student success*, National Postsecondary Education Cooperative. https://nces.ed.gov/npec/pdf/kuh_team_report.pdf

Kutieleh, S., Morgan, D. L. & Egege, Y. S. (2004). To stay or not to stay: Factors affecting international and Indigenous students' decisions to persist with university study and the implications for support services. In K. Deller-Evans & P. Zeegers (Eds.), *Refereed proceedings of the 2003 Biennial language and academic skills in higher education conference* (pp. 89–98). Flinders University.

Lau, K. (2017). 'The most important things is to learn the way to learn': Evaluating the effectiveness of independent learning by perceptual changes. *Assessment and Evaluation in Higher Education, 42*(3), 415–430. DOI: 10.1080/02602938.2015.1118434

Lemmens, J.-C. (2011). *Students' readiness for university education* [PhD thesis, University of Pretoria]. https://hdl.handle.net/2263/26675

Leveson, L., McNeil, N. & Joiner, T. (2013). Persist or withdraw: The importance of external factors in students' departure intentions. *Higher Education Research & Development, 32*(6), 932–945. https://doi.org/10.1080/07294360.2013.806442

Linnenbrink, E. A. & Pintrich, Paul P. R. (2002). Motivation as an enabler for academic success. *School Psychology Review, 31*(3), 313–327. https://doi.org/10.1080/02796015.2002.12086158

Lipman, S. (2015). *Student Perceptions of College Readiness: An Examination of the Processes that Impact Factors of Psychosocial Development.* [PhD thesis, California State University, Northbridge].https://scholarworks.csun.edu/bitstream/handle/10211.3/152203/Lipman-Sivan-thesis-2015.pdf?sequence=1

Martin, G., Nakata, V., Nakata, M. & Day, A. (2017). Promoting the persistence of Indigenous students through teaching at the Cultural Interface. *Studies in Higher Education, 42*(7), 1158–1173. https://doi.org/10.1080/03075079.2015.1083001

Masika, R. & Jones, J. (2016). Building student belonging and engagement: Insights into higher education students' experiences of participating and learning together. *Teaching in Higher Education, 21*(2), 138–150. https://doi.org/10.1080/13562517.2015.1122585

McCombs, B. L. & Marzano, R. J. (1990). Putting the self in self-regulated learning: The self as agent in integrating will and skill. *Educational Psychologist, 25*(1), 51–69. https://psycnet.apa.org/doi/10.1207/s15326985ep2501_5

McInnes, C. (2003, August 24–27). *New realities of the student experience: How should universities respond?* [Conference presentation]. *25th Annual Conference, European Association of Institutional Research*, University of Limerick, Ireland.

McKendry, S. & Boyd, V. (2012). Defining the independent learner in UK Higher Education: staff and students' understanding of the concept. *International Journal of Teaching and Learning in Higher Education, 24*(2), 209–220. https://eric.ed.gov/?id=EJ996267

Meyer, W. R. (2010, September 1–4). *Independent learning: A literature review and a new project* [Conference presentation]. British Educational Research Association Annual Conference, University of Warwick, England. https://mkx20bvs5a2cy6u43bq2jqtp-wpengine.netdna-ssl.com/wp-content/uploads/2016/06/Independent-learning-review.pdf

Nakata, M. (2007). *Disciplining the savages, savaging the disciplines.* Aboriginal Studies Press.

Nakata, M., Nakata, V. & Chin, M. (2008). Approaches to the academic support of Australian Indigenous students for tertiary studies. *Australian Journal of Indigenous Education, 37*(S1), 137–145. https://doi.org/10.1375/S1326011100000478

Nakata, M., Nakata, V., Day, A. & Peachey, M. (2019a). Closing gaps in Indigenous undergraduate higher education outcomes: Repositioning the role of student support services to improve retention and completion rates. *Australian Journal of Indigenous Education, 48*(1), 1–11. https://doi.org/10.1017/jie.2017.36

Nakata, M., Nakata, V., Day, A., Martin, G. & Peachey, M. (2019b). Indigenous undergraduates' use of supplementary tutors: Developing academic capabilities for success in higher education studies. *Australian Journal of Indigenous Education, 48*(2), 119–128. https://doi.org/10.1017/jie.2017.39

Nelson, K., Kift, S. & Clarke, J. (2012). A transition pedagogy for student engagement and first-year learning, success and retention. In A. Reid, P. Petocz & I. Solomonides (Eds.), *Engaging with learning in higher education* (pp. 117–144). Libri Publishing.

O'Donnell, V., Kean, M. & Stevens, G. (2016). *Student transition in higher education: Concepts, theories and practices.* Higher Education Academy.

Oliver, R., Grote, E., Rochecouste, J. & Dann, T. (2016). Indigenous student perspectives on support and impediments at university. *Australian Journal of Indigenous Education, 45*(1), 23–35. https://doi.org/10.1017/jie.2015.16

Oliver, R., Rochecouste, J., Bennell, D., Anderson, R., Cooper, I., Forrest, S. & Exell, M. (2013b). Understanding Australian Aboriginal tertiary student needs. *International Journal of Higher Education, 2*(4), 52–64. https://doi.org/10.5430/ijhe.v2n4p52

Oliver, R., Rochecouste, J. & Grote, E. (2013a). *The transition of Aboriginal and Torres Strait Islander students into higher education.* Office for Learning and Teaching. https://ltr.edu.au/resources/SI11_2137_Oliver_Report_2013.pdf

Orygen, The National Centre of Excellence in Youth Mental Health. (2017). *Under the radar: The mental health of university students.* https://www.orygen.org.au/Policy/Policy-Reports/Under-the-radar/Orygen-Under_the_radar_report?ext

Page, S., DiGregorio, K. D. & Farrington, S. (1997, November 30–December 4). *The student experiences study: Understanding the factors that affect Aboriginal and Torres Strait Islander students' academic success* [Conference presentation]. Annual Conference of the Australian Association for Research in Education, Brisbane, Australia. https://www.aare.edu.au/data/publications/1997/digrk446.pdf

Pajares, F. (1996). Self-efficacy beliefs in academic settings. *Review of Educational Research, 66*(4), 543–578. https://doi.org/10.3102%2F00346543066004543

Paris, S. G. & Winograd, P. (2003). *The role of self-regulated learning in contextual teaching: Principles and practices for teacher preparation. A commissioned paper for the U.S. Department of Education project* Preparing teachers to use contextual teaching and learning strategies to improve student success in and beyond school. Office of Educational Research and Improvement. https://files.eric.ed.gov/fulltext/ED479905.pdf

Pascarella, E. T. & Terenzini, P. T. (2005). *How college affects students: A third decade of research* (Vol. 2). Jossey-Bass.

Pechenkina, E. (2019). Persevering, educating and influencing a change: A case study of Australian Aboriginal and Torres Strait Islander narratives of academic success. *Critical Studies in Education, 60*(4), 496–512. https://doi.org/10.1080/17508487.2017.1309327

Pekrun, R., Goetz, T., Titz, W. & Perry, R. P. (2002). Academic emotions in students' self-regulated learning and achievement: A program of qualitative and quantitative research. *Educational Psychologist, 37*(2), 91–105. https://doi.org/10.1207/S15326985EP3702_4

Puustinen, M. & Pulkkinen, L. (2001). Models of self-regulated learning: A review. *Scandinavian Journal of Educational Research, 45*(3), 269–286. https://doi.org/10.1080/00313830120074206

Quality Indicators for Learning and Teaching. (2018, March). 2017 *Student experience survey: National report.* https://www.qilt.edu.au/qilt-surveys/student-experience

Read, B., Archer, L. & Leathwood, C. (2003). Challenging cultures? Student conceptions of 'belonging' and 'isolation' at a post-1992 university. *Studies in Higher Education, 28*(3), 261–277. https://doi.org/10.1080/03075070309290

Reason, R. D. (2009). An examination of persistence research through the lens of a comprehensive conceptual framework. *Journal of College Student Development, 50*(6), 659–682. https://psycnet.apa.org/doi/10.1353/csd.0.0098

Reeves, T. D. & Stich, A. E. (2011). Tackling suboptimal bachelor's degree completion rates through training in self-regulated learning (SRL). *Innovative Higher Education, 36*(1), 3–17. https://doi.org/10.1007/s10755-010-9152-x

Rigney, L.-I. & Neill, B. (2018, June). *Higher education outcomes for Indigenous Australians: Barriers and enablers to participation and completion.* Centre for Research in Social Inclusion and Education. https://apo.org.au/sites/default/files/resource-files/2018-06/apo-nid201806.pdf

Robbins, S., Lauver, K., Le, H., Davis, D., Langley, R. & Carlstrom, A. (2004). Do psychosocial and study skills factors predict college outcomes? A meta-analysis. *Psychological Bulletin, 130*(2), 261–268. https://doi.org/10.1037/0033-2909.130.2.261

Roth, A., Ogrin, S. & Schmitz, B. (2016). Assessing self-regulated learning in higher education: A systematic literature review of self-report instruments. *Educational Assessment, Evaluation and Accountability, 28*(3), 225–250. https://psycnet.apa.org/doi/10.1007/s11092-015-9229-2

Russell, L. & Jarvis, C. (2019). Student withdrawal, retention and their sense of belonging: Their experience in their words. *Research in Educational Administration & Leadership, 4*(3), 494–525. https://doi.org/.30828/real/2019.3.3

Ryan, R. M. & Deci, E. L. (2000a). Intrinsic and extrinsic motivations: Classic definitions and new directions. *Contemporary Educational Psychology, 25*(1), 54–67. https://doi.org/10.1006/ceps.1999.1020

Ryan, R. M. & Deci, E. L. (2000b). Self-determination theory and the facilitation of intrinsic motivation, social development, and well-being. *American Psychologist, 55*(1), 68–78. https://doi.apa.org/doi/10.1037/0003-066X.55.1.68

Schunk, D. H. (1990). Goal setting and self-efficacy during self-regulated learning. *Educational Psychologist, 25*(1), 71–86. https://doi.org/10.1207/s15326985ep2501_6

Schunk, D. H. (2005). Self-regulated learning: The educational legacy of Paul R. Pintrich. *Educational Psychologist, 40*(2), 85–94. https://doi.org/10.1207/s15326985ep4002_3

Schunk, D. H. & Zimmerman, B. J. (2006). Competence and control beliefs: Distinguishing the means and ends. In P. A. Alexander & P. H. Winnie (Eds.), *Handbook of educational psychology* (2nd ed., pp. 349–367). Lawrence Erlbaum Associates.

Schuster, C., Stebner, F., Leutner, D. & Wirth, J. (2020). Transfer of metacognitive skills in self-regulated learning: An experimental training study. *Metacognition Learning, 15*, 455–477. https://doi.org/10.1007/s11409-020-09237-5

Schwartz, M. (2018). Retaining our best: Imposter syndrome, cultural safety, complex lives and Indigenous student experiences of law school. *Legal Education Review, 28*(2), 1–22. https://doi.org/10.53300/001c.7455

Stallman, H. M. (2010). Psychological distress in university students: A comparison with general population data. *Australian Psychologist, 45*(4), 249–257. https://doi.org/10.1080/00050067.2010.482109

Taylor, E. V., Lalovic, A. & Thompson, S. C. (2019). Beyond enrolments: A systematic review exploring the factors affecting the retention of Aboriginal and Torres Strait Islander health students in the tertiary education system. *International Journal for Equity Health, 18*(1), Article 136. https://doi.org/10.1186/s12939-019-1038-7

Terenzini, P. T. & Pascarella, E. T. (1991). Twenty years of research on college students: Lessons for future research. *Research in Higher Education, 32*(1), 83–92. https://doi.org/10.1007/BF00992835

The University of Melbourne. (2016.) A Framework for Promoting Student Mental Wellbeing in Universities. https://unistudentwellbeing.edu.au/wp-content/uploads/2016/11/MCSHE-Student-Wellbeing-Framework_FINAL.pdf

The University of Sydney. (2019, October 2). *What is mental health?* https://www.sydney. edu.au/news-opinion/news/2019/10/02/what-is-mental-health.html

The University of Sydney. (2020). *Student Mental Wellbeing Strategy.* https://www.sydney. edu.au/content/dam/corporate/documents/about-us/values-and-visions/student_ mental_wellbeing_strategy.pdf

Thomas, L. (2012, July). *Building student engagement and belonging in higher education at a time of change: Final report from the What Works? Student Retention & Success programme.* Paul Hamlyn Foundation; Action on Access; Higher Education Funding Council for England; Higher Education Academy. https://www.advance-he.ac.uk/knowledge-hub/building-student-engagement-and-belonging-higher-education-time-change-final-report

Tinto, V. (1975). Dropout from higher education: A theoretical synthesis of recent research. *Review of Educational Research, 45*(1), 89–125. https://doi.org/10.3102/00346543045001089

Tinto, V. (2005). Reflections on retention and persistence: Institutional actions on behalf of student persistence. *Studies in Learning, Evaluation, Innovation and Development, 2*(3), 89–97.

Tinto, V. (2012). Enhancing student success: Taking the classroom success seriously. *International Journal of the First Year in Higher Education, 3*(1), 1–8. https://doi.org/10.5204/ intjfyhe.v3i1.119

Tinto, V. (2015). Through the eyes of students. *Journal of College Student Retention: Research, Theory & Practice, 19*(3), 254–269. https://doi.org/10.1177%2F1521025115621917

Toombs, M. & Gorman, D. (2011). Mental health and Indigenous university students. *Aboriginal and Islander Health Worker Journal, 35*(4), 22–24. https://core.ac.uk/download/ pdf/11047691.pdf

Trigwell, K., Ellis, R. A. & Han, F. (2012). Relations between students' approaches to learning, experienced emotions and outcomes of learning. *Studies in Higher Education, 37*(7), 811–824. https://doi.org/10.1080/03075079.2010.549220

Trowler, P. & Trowler, V. (2010, November). *Frameworks for action: Enhancing student engagement at the institutional level.* Higher Education Academy. https://www.heacademy.ac.uk/ sites/default/files/resources/Frameworkforaction_institutional.pdf

Trowler, V. (2010, November). *Student engagement literature review.* Higher Education academy. https://www.heacademy.ac.uk/system/files/StudentEngagementLiteratureReview_1.pdf

Universities Australia. (2017). At a glance: The 2017 Universities Australia student finances survey. https://www.universitiesaustralia.edu.au/wp-content/uploads/2019/06/Student-Finances-Survey-Factsheet.pdf

van Breda, A. D. (2018). A critical review of resilience theory and its relevance for social work. *Social Work/Maatskaplike Werk, 54*(1), 1–18. https://doi.org/10.15270/54-1-611

Walker, R. (2000). *Indigenous performance in Western Australia universities: Reframing retention and success.* Commonwealth Department of Education, Training and Youth Affairs. https://www.voced.edu.au/content/ngv%3A61280#

Zepke, N. (2013). Student engagement: A complex business supporting the first year experience in tertiary education. *International Journal of the First Year in Higher Education, 4*(2), 1–14. https://doi.org/10.5204/intjfyhe.v4i2.183

Zepke, N. (2014). Student engagement research in higher education: Questioning an academic orthodoxy. *Teaching in Higher Education, 19*(6), 697–708. https://doi.org/10.1080 /13562517.2014.901956

Zepke, N., Butler, P. & Leach, L. (2012). Institutional research and improving the quality of student engagement. *Quality in Higher Education, 18*(3), 329–347. https://doi.org/10. 1080/13538322.2012.730338

Zepke, N., Leach, L. & Butler, P. (2010a). Student engagement: What is it and what influences it? *Teaching & Learning Research Initiative.* https://www.tlri.org.nz/sites/default/files/projects/9261-Introduction.pdf

Zepke, N., Leach, L. & Butler, P. (2010b). Engagement in post-compulsory education: Students' motivation and action. *Research in Post-Compulsory Education, 15*(1), 1–17. https://doi.org/10.1080/13596740903565269

Zepke, N., Leach, L. & Prebble, T. (2006). Being learner centred: One way to improve student retention? *Studies in Higher Education, 31*(5), 587–600. https://doi.org/10.1080/03075070600923418

Zimmerman, B. J. (1990). Self-regulated learning and academic achievement: An overview. *Educational Psychologist, 25*, 3–17.

Zimmerman, B. J., Bonner, S. & Kovach, R. (1996). *Developing self-regulated learners: Beyond achievement to self-efficacy.* American Psychological Association.

Zimmermann, B. J. (2002). Becoming a self-regulated learner: An overview. *Theory Into Practice, 41*(2), 64–70. https://doi.org/10.1207/s15430421tip4102_2

2 An individual student case management approach

This chapter sets out the essential elements of an individual student case management approach for Indigenous student support through a focus on the 'what and how' of support staff's everyday practices. The chapter draws on the knowledge explored in Chapter 1, as well as insights from students and lessons from our reform experience over ten years in two universities: a Group of Eight university in a major city and a regional university. We discuss some basic considerations and issues to consider when developing support systems and processes for monitoring and tracking student progress and provide some examples of practice from our experiences in two universities. Knowing, understanding, monitoring, and tracking individual students' needs, progress (including their movements towards independent learning), and outcomes are central to a capacity development approach for Indigenous student support and success. While the rhetoric of monitoring and tracking is now part of the Indigenous student support discourse, there is little guidance for support managers and staff about how to develop systems to enable and manage individual support for all students and the day-to-day workload involved. This chapter aims to fill this gap.

Developing student profiles: Why, what, and when to collect student information

Information about students is central to any monitoring process and student case management system. Assessing students' circumstances and likely challenges and support needs is the basis for support staff activities that are responsive to an individual student's needs. Student profile information is the foundational basis of knowledge about individual students. Establishing a student profile for every student is the first step in building a monitoring and tracking system. This provides the starting point for assessing the likely extent of a student's need for support and the areas where a student is likely to need support or assistance.

Ideally, profile information about students begins with the first contact with a student and is continuously updated throughout the student's educational journey. First contact might be through outreach activities in schools or communities, pre-entry activities in universities, or tertiary admission centre databases (prospective students). A prospective student profile might include contact details, schools, year level, educational and work attainments, prospective course interests, and

DOI: 10.4324/9781003326458-3

career aspirations. Any insights about student attributes, extracurricular experiences, strengths, talents, and areas of under-preparedness are useful to collect at the pre-entry stage. Information gathering at this stage enables staff to remain in contact with prospective students. It also helps staff begin to consider and distribute useful information and advice to prospective students prior to offers, acceptances, or enrolments. This contact and interest by staff is an additional recruitment tool for building students' confidence and feelings of being valued. The information gained (as it becomes available) through prospective students' participation in alternative selection-for-entry diagnostic testing and interviews, tertiary rankings, and relevant year 12 subjects and results should also be used to inform student profiles.

Once a student is enrolled, profile information can be consolidated and updated as they progress through their course of study. Relevant information for understanding commencing and continuing students' needs for guidance and their likely academic and support needs include contact details, prior educational attainments, years since last formal study, course and subject enrolments, course year level, part-time/full-time status, mode of study, age and gender, first-in-family status, accommodation, away from home status (especially if young and away from home for the first time), daily commute times to university, remote/regional status, financial situation, employment status/hours, levels of family and other obligations and health, wellbeing, or disability needs.

This information should be collected and updated systematically and as early as possible for all students if it is to be useful for staff planning. Early planning by support staff might include, for example, identifying vulnerable or at-risk students as a priority; determining students' likely academic support needs by assessing the demands of courses and subjects they are enrolled in against their prior educational attainments; identifying students who need financial and accommodation assistance and providing that assistance early, in time for commencing study; determining the circumstances and social support networks of students, especially young students away from home for the first time, to assess their needs for social support; identifying any commencing students who will not know anyone in their course and determining their other peer and social supports; communicating with students with other obligations to determine what sort of support would be helpful (e.g., mature-age, working, single parents, or external or remote learning students).

A simple system for identifying individual students' likely support needs is a traffic light system developed at our previous university. This uses student information to flag whether a student is likely to need intensive, moderate, or minimal levels of support: a red flag is assigned if a student is assessed as likely to struggle or is struggling; a yellow flag is assigned if a student is assessed as likely to cope reasonably well or is coping reasonably well but requires regular assistance and support or intensive support in one particular area; and a green flag is assigned if a student is assessed as not likely to need much support or need only occasional support. Students can also be flagged for other criteria and at the cohort level, for example, to flag students who are not in good standing or are enrolled in a subject known to have a high failure rate. Flags can help staff set priorities for monitoring students.

Early planning enables staff to consider what they need to do to ensure that commencing and continuing students have the support they need to be organised and sufficiently resourced by the beginning of the semester. Keeping student profile information up to date is essential to stay abreast of students' changing needs.

Using student information to assess students' support needs and develop individual learning support plans

Student information serves little purpose unless used or acted on, first, as a basis for staff assessments of each student's likely support needs and, second, to enable staff to consider how best to support those needs. The question is: how should staff do this in practice for large cohorts of students?

One method used by the staff in our current support centre is to construct individual learning support plans (ILSPs) for each student in a team's cohort. ILSPs link the student profile information and proactive approaches to providing individual support. These plans are simple and brief and describe the main strengths or areas of concern about a student and what staff intend to do to ensure the student is supported in these areas during the semester. The plan includes references to either or both academic and personal areas depending on a student's academic history or personal profile. Academic and pastoral support advisers construct ILSPs together by assessing the relevant profile and accumulated information to identify areas of risk, vulnerability, or opportunity (for students with particular strengths). Staff consider each student's educational background, diagnostic results, previous semester results, subject enrolments, and relevant personal issues to develop the plan. When academic and pastoral support team members set these plans together, they develop a fuller understanding of a student's challenges and a greater awareness of intersecting issues.

Initially, establishing these plans is likely to be time-consuming. if each team's student cohort comprises approximately 130 students each, as they do in our current university, where each support team comprises one academic support officer and one pastoral support officer. However, staff teams become more efficient at setting initial plans for students with practice, and the task becomes easier as staff become acquainted with students through regular contact and monitoring. Typically, ILSPs begin with only two or three actions. For example, the ILSP for an underprepared student undertaking a maths subject who does not know anyone in her course and does not have financial stability might include: 'organise maths tutor from week one for subject X and regularly check on progress; ensure she is connected to other students in her course before commencement; check needs for social support; keep checking on the progress of her finance.' For high achieving or relatively independent students, an initial ILSP might note: 'discuss how often X wants to be contacted; check on any challenges or anxieties; alert them to the availability of tutors; emphasise they can contact us at any time.' It is important to explain the concept of ILSPs carefully to staff. Confusion can arise if the purposes and formats of these plans are not well conveyed. ILSPs are *not* detailed remedial-type plans for students to follow. They do not set tasks for students to do. They are fundamentally brief references to issues for support staff to check or explore with students and/or a prompt for staff actions and follow-ups. They are set up at the start of each semester. They cannot be detailed because the purpose is to provide active support, not overly consume staff time with written plans. Staff mostly use bullet points and note forms rather than elaborated sentences. At the end of the semester, staff review students' ILSPs in the context of their results and challenges during the semester. On this basis, they initiate new individual plans for the coming semester. Staff interactions and interventions with students during the semester are recorded elsewhere through a different process.[1] However, unless there is a written plan at the beginning of the semester, it is easy for staff to forget individual students' initial identified needs and fail to attend to some students' needs. Because developing these plans does require time, managers have a role in ensuring staff set aside sufficient time to plan and provide some oversight to ensure staff are completing ILSPs.

ILSP development is a professional development area for all staff and for new staff that can be managed through staff meetings, workshops, or induction processes. Semester review points should include opportunities for staff to reflect on how well plans worked and how they can be improved to be more effective. Because an ILSP includes academic and pastoral support actions, both team members have opportunities to integrate their efforts when responding to individual students with complex and intersecting needs.

Developing contact strategies to monitor student needs over the semester

Monitoring and tracking rely on more than just baseline profile knowledge about students and initial action plans. Effective monitoring and tracking depend on knowing how students are managing at any point in time. Given that many Indigenous students who could benefit from more support do not seek assistance, a regular strategy for interacting with students is essential for effectively monitoring and tracking students' progress and needs throughout their studies. While whole-of-cohort emails have their place and purpose, they are not sufficient for monitoring and tracking. A sound monitoring strategy is systemised rather than random. That is, contact should not simply occur when staff have some spare time or think about how a particular student is managing. Rather, as part of sound individual case management, a contact strategy should be planned in advance and involve contacting all students during a set period and at planned intervals. This does not mean that staff should not interact with students at other times. Regular contact helps identify issues that require ongoing follow-ups and contact outside these scheduled times.

The elements of a student contact strategy will depend on the specific student support context and cohort characteristics, which vary across universities. This section describes the strategy used by staff in our current university, a regional university with a history of low Indigenous student outcomes on the comparative national scale. Although support staff have been in contact with students prior to commencement and orientation week, the student contact strategy requires support staff to contact all students in their cohort in teaching weeks three, six, nine, and twelve to ascertain how students are managing.

The engagement technique used at these contact points is called TAPS, which prompts staff to make four broad enquiries about the student's *transition* (i.e., how are they settling in?), *academic* needs (i.e., how are they managing in their subjects?), *pastoral* needs (i.e., do they have any personal challenges, e.g., finance, accommodation, wellbeing, or time issues?), and *support* needs (i.e., do they need any specific guidance or assistance?). During the first TAPS call, students are asked for their preferred mode of contact—phone or email—and are given the option not to be contacted or to set a longer period between calls. However, commencing students and students known to be struggling or experiencing regular subject failures are strongly encouraged to engage in TAPS sessions during weeks three, six, nine, and twelve and to respond to staff whenever contacted. It is also accepted that higher-achieving students and more independent students need less contact than others, but these students are still monitored behind the scenes through institutional sources of student outcomes and learning engagement information, although many are happy to be contacted occasionally or by email rather than phone. One student we interviewed said that even though they did not need support, it was affirming to have their achievements acknowledged by staff, and they appreciated post-results contact.

Both members of the teams share the load, which is time-intensive. They note student responses/issues for follow-up by the appropriate team member. The TAPS strategy is an adaptation of the contact strategy developed at our previous university. Known as PATS, it asked the same questions related to *pastoral, academic, transition,* and *support* issues but contacted all students during the first few weeks of each semester, before the census date. During the first semester that it was trialled, the attrition rate was greatly reduced compared to the first semester in the previous year. During the remaining weeks of the semester, the staff engaged in follow-up activities.

Staff in our current university also do several things to prepare for their TAPS calls. The staff review their previous contact session notes and suggestions to review how students are now managing a previously reported issue and examine the students' use of the university's learning management system and any assessment outcomes. This provides an idea of how the students are engaging and whether they are making progress. It also provides talking points for interactions with reluctant students or students who say that everything is fine (as many do when things are actually not going well). It is important that these interactions enable students to feel they have a supporter in their corner and are not being called out.

Proactive contact with students can be intrusive if mishandled. Thus, the ethics, language, and disposition of staff approaches to students is an important area of professional development, as are the methods for maintaining the privacy and confidentiality of all students.

Regular contact aims to help students before they experience so much difficulty that their chances of success are threatened. However, it is important at the same time that students develop their help-seeking behaviours and gain the confidence to ask for help on their own initiative because the ability to seek help when needed is a characteristic of independent learners. In our case management system, help-seeking behaviour is a measure that staff can track on the 'movement towards independence' scale. Methods for encouraging help-seeking behaviour are discussed more broadly in Chapter 3.

Daily workloads and individual staff task lists

Direct and regular contact with students adds to staff knowledge about how their students manage their learning and the other aspects of their lives that influence their learning outcomes. However, this information must also be acted upon. Following TAPS sessions, staff need to set their own tasks for following up on identified student needs. With an average of 130 students to manage, staff require a well-defined process to achieve this. Thus, when individual student issues are identified through staff–student interactions during TAPS sessions, a separate task for each student issue that requires *action* by staff should be set. Support staff tasks or actions should be subject to a triage process. They should be diarised according to the type or urgency of a student's needs rather than addressed student by student, which could leave some students with urgent issues receiving assistance too late. Pastoral support staff should respond to personal issues; academic support staff to learning issues.

Under each diarised task, staff should enter case notes, providing additional information regarding the student's issue and how the staff member responded. These notes should continue while the student needs support and follow-up or as new issues arise. Task lists and notes should include all interactions with students, whether through TAPS, emails, or face-to-face interactions at any time during the semester. Staff should also continue to add to the notes or profiles any new information that helps them understand their students but does not require actions by the staff. Thus, there is a task list set following every staff–student interaction and this should provide a chronological record of staff actions alongside student issues.

Maintaining accurate student histories helps staff keep abreast of student needs and challenges and preserves information that might help students make a case regarding their academic standing or personal circumstances. These daily task lists are separate from ILSP entries, which remain stable throughout a semester, with adjustments for the next semester. If there are no organised daily task lists, it is very easy for individual student needs to go unaddressed and for staff to fail to use the information gathered through the student monitoring process effectively. Because managing staff–student interactions and task lists is a complex process, our current university subscribes to *the WillowSoft Student Success Platform for Indigenous students*,[2] which streamlines this process to help staff manage individual cases. The system automatically maintains a dated record of staff contact and actions.

Tracking student movements towards independent learning

If one of the goals of student support is to ensure students develop the capabilities of independent learners over time, then a process for tracking this development needs to be considered. One simple method is to use a traffic light system and update the flags according to how frequently students require support and how intensively the support was provided.[3] This update can also be based on the information gained from student contact sessions (i.e., TAPS) and measured against student outcomes. However, the red, yellow, and green flags do not capture the more incremental steps students often make on their way to independence. In our current university, we use a 5-point scale, similar to a Likert scale. The 5-point scale comprises the following stages: 1 = student struggling and not seeking support or responding to staff contact; 2 = student struggling but seeking assistance and support; 3 = student coping and making progress but still requires regular support; 4 = student managing well most of the time, with support when needed; 5 = student managing very well and rarely requires support.

Scales that only measure a student's academic outcomes against how frequently they have required support miss the chance to measure how individual students are performing with regard to the different sorts of skills, study behaviours, and wellbeing factors associated with successful independent learning. To gain more insight into the areas in which individual students struggle to manage without support, we constructed measures for the three main student capacity areas necessary for success: academic learning, student wellbeing, and finance. The key influences associated with student success were identified within these areas based on the research regarding Indigenous academic persistence and the key concepts associated with student success.[4] These key influences form the measures. For example, some of the measures we are currently using include self-efficacy; self-regulation; motivation and goal setting; persistence and resilience; use of enabling skills workshops; student engagement; self-organisation; using a tutor; help-seeking behaviour; health and wellbeing; managing emotions; study resources; and finance.

Staff establish the students' status when they commence their studies and only adjust these as students progress towards being more independent. This task is made possible by the student case management system we use, which allows staff to assess students using the scales; students to self-report against these measures; and tutors to assess students on any measure relevant to their knowledge of the student's progress. Discrepancies between these assessments alert staff to investigate further; for example, a student who scores themselves highly on 'engagement,' when support staff know they are not attending lectures and/or tutorials, may still be engaging with tasks but need support to manage face-to-face learning, or they may be struggling and feel unable to ask for help.

While this measurement system seems complicated, it becomes more routine and quicker to manage as staff become familiar with it and their students. Using these scales will require initial professional development through staff meetings or induction processes.

Monitoring students' use and effectiveness of supplementary tutoring

Supplementary tutors are critical to many Indigenous students' chances of success.[5] Monitoring students' use and the effectiveness of one-to-one supplementary tutoring is particularly important in contexts where tutors or tutor hours are underused, when students who use tutors are not using them effectively or when tutors and students do not work well together. To do this, it helps to advise students that their challenges or performance indicates that they should use a supplementary tutor. It also helps to know which students are using tutors and ask them (during TAPS sessions) how their work with tutors is progressing so that interventions can be made to help the process, including giving a student a different tutor, if necessary. Having a way to receive feedback from tutors can also present another perspective of the working relationship between students and tutors. When asked about their irregular attendance to supplementary tutorial sessions or failure to advise tutors when they cannot make a session, students have been known to blame the tutor rather than their own disorganisation or lack of commitment. An easy method for soliciting feedback from tutors is to create a section on tutors' electronic pay application forms so they can add comments about the progress of their sessions. We also use an electronic feedback form that students and tutors can fill out. Academic support advisers should ensure that students who need tutors get them, that the student–tutor relationship is working, and that the student is benefiting from the way they are using their tutors.

Using local data to improve support strategies and practices

Local data analysis is a valuable source of information for reviewing and improving support strategies and practices. The more analysis is conducted, the more is revealed about the areas where students are having difficulties or doing well. This sort of knowledge assists student support staff to review the areas of concern where a more focused support effort is indicated for students. This might include concerns about student achievement outcomes at particular stages of their educational journey, in particular disciplines or courses, subjects, skills, and support areas (e.g., finance, social, or academic support). Such a review then prompts discussions about the effectiveness/shortfalls of current strategies and any impediments that might prevent students from taking advantage of the support, including logistical issues and staff and student practices. In our previous university, we began with dedicated staff review and planning days at the end of the year. In our current university, these review points are held at the end of each semester. The most important information to analyse is student outcomes data. This section provides some examples of the sorts of analyses that are beneficial, if not essential to good support practice.

The first four examples (see Figures 2.1–2.4) illustrate some aspects of student progress during a semester, which are included in student support teams' end-of-semester reports. Each support team presents a report to all support staff during dedicated planning days. Staff reports have become more sophisticated over the four years staff have been producing them, aided by the WillowSoft case management software program.[6] Their reports variously include statistical information (usually graphed) regarding various combinations of the following data: the breakdown of their cohort numbers to indicate how many students are in each of the disciplines they manage; numbers of subject fails, passes, credits, distinctions, and high distinctions; numbers of students in each GPA level; student academic standing data; and numbers of students who used supplementary tutors and the hours of tutoring their students used. Staff sometimes analyse this data to provide this information according to the specific disciplinary cohorts and year levels, in which their students study. They also compare semester-specific data to either the previous semester or the previous year. Some teams have begun to report examples of the outcomes of staff interventions for individual students whose personal challenges place them at risk of failure or withdrawal. These examples remind all staff of the importance of timely intervention and the information and professional networks needed to resolve situations quickly. The staff then discuss what they think is working, the areas that require attention, and their improvement plans for the following semester. This enables analyses of the effects of any strategic changes to services and unforeseen factors, such as COVID-19.

Figure 2.1, for example, shows how one team represented an overview of the academic standing status of their cohort and the grades they achieved. The graph shows the total cohort number of students (129) that the team is responsible for supporting. The bars indicate the courses these students are taking and the numbers of students taking each one. The bars are colour coded and numbered to show how many students are considered 'at risk,' how many have been given 'conditional' status, and how many are in 'good standing.' The other graphs in Figure 2.1 delve a bit deeper into students' grades, allowing staff to see not just how well some students are doing but where they need to further investigate the reasons for unsatisfactory outcomes and the implications for improving support and following up with students who are not at good standing.

Figures 2.2 and 2.3 illustrate what an analysis of the most frequently failed subjects can reveal and the implications for supporting students who undertake these subjects in the future. For example, Figure 2.2 is a bar graph that represents the 11 most frequently failed subjects between 2015 and 2019 out of the 1330 subjects that Indigenous students undertook. (The subjects have been de-identified for this book but are clearly identified for support staff.) Support staff in our current university call these subjects 'grief subjects' and some of them are hurdle subjects that must be passed to progress. A retrospective analysis of these 11 subjects revealed that they resulted in 900 failures out of a total of 4300 subject failures between 2015 and 2019, which means that 20% of subject failures came from 0.8% of the subjects undertaken. A proportion of these most frequently failed subjects were math subjects or subjects that had a math component, confirming the challenges that underprepared Indigenous students face in courses that require competencies in maths. Seeing these figures led to support staff teams, who had students taking those subjects in the future, to provide very close monitoring and tracking and to ensure those students had supplementary tutors allocated to them.

Figure 2.3 is a bar graph that shows the trend in students' results in these 11 subjects following closer attention and support to students undertaking them in the years. The vertical axis indicates the percentage of students, with the horizontal bar indicating a range of results outcomes, which from left to right denote those students being given Supplementary exams or assessments and Fails, and those achieving Pass, Credit, Distinction, and High Distinction levels. For each of these grades, a series of dark grey, light grey and white bars denotes the percentage of students achieving these grades in 2017, 2018, and 2019, respectively. In

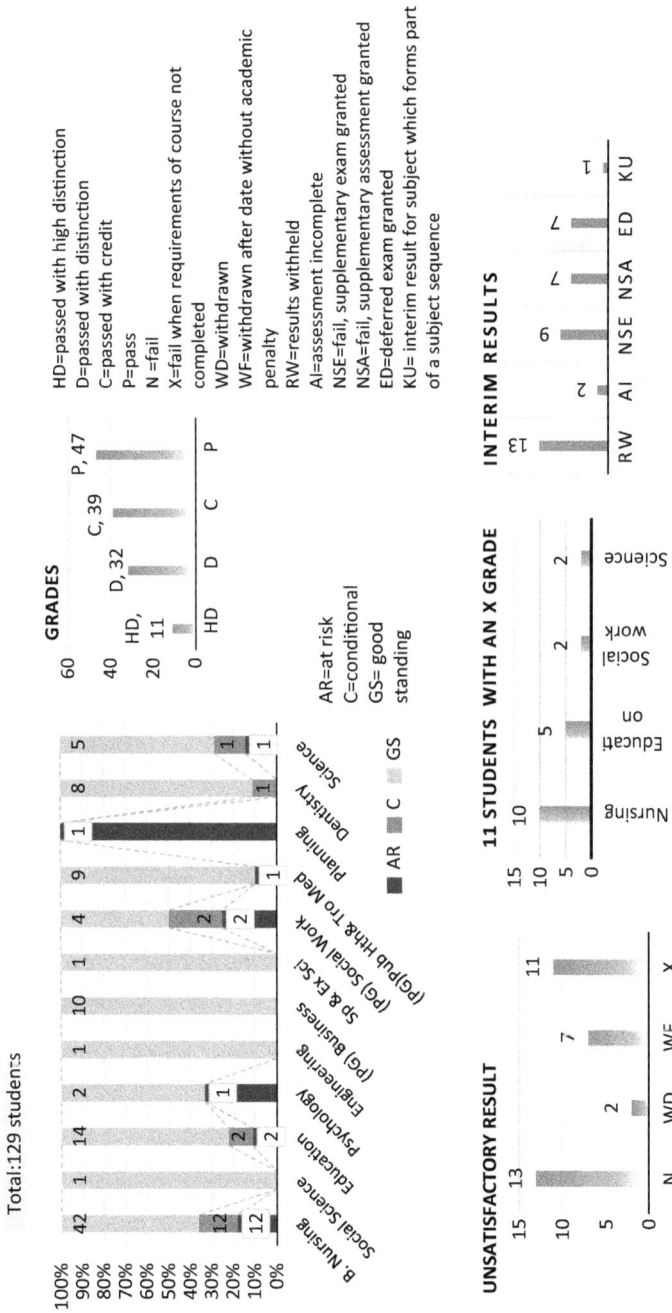

Figure 2.1 Graphs of student academic standing and semester results

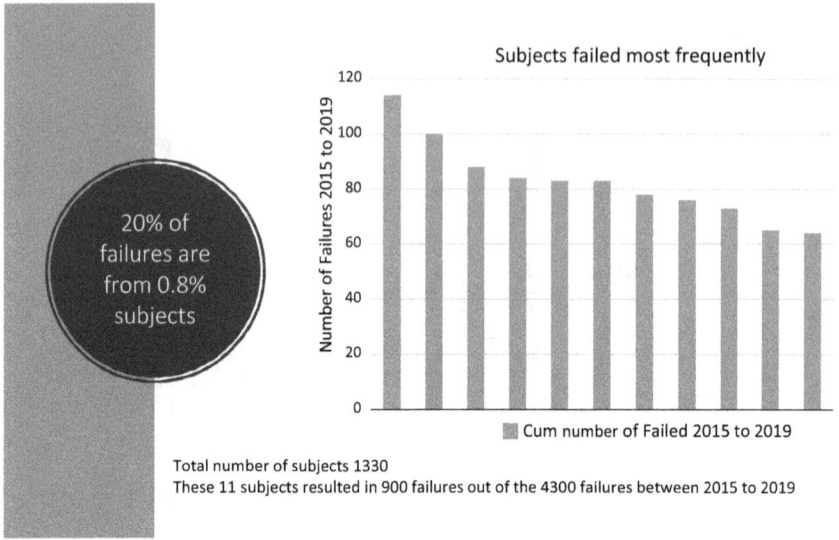

Subjects failed most frequently

20% of failures are from 0.8% subjects

Total number of subjects 1330
These 11 subjects resulted in 900 failures out of the 4300 failures between 2015 to 2019

Figure 2.2 Graph of the 11 'grief subjects'

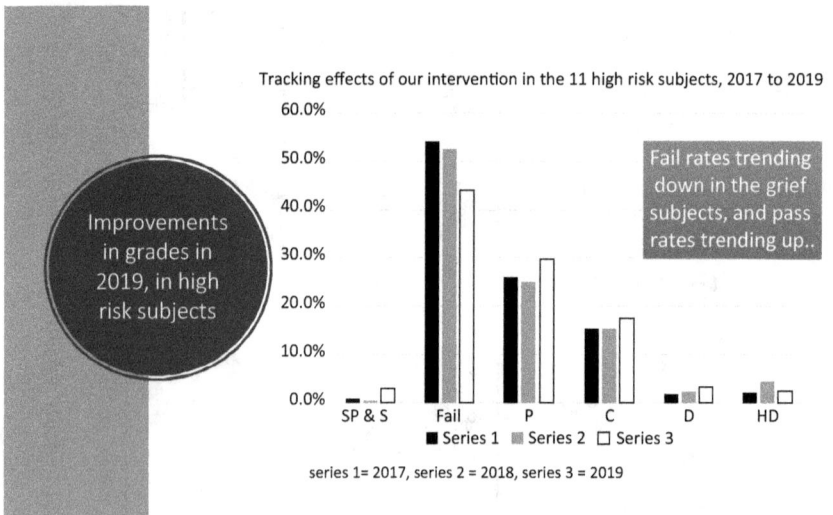

Tracking effects of our intervention in the 11 high risk subjects, 2017 to 2019

Improvements in grades in 2019, in high risk subjects

Fail rates trending down in the grief subjects, and pass rates trending up..

■ Series 1 ■ Series 2 □ Series 3

series 1= 2017, series 2 = 2018, series 3 = 2019

Figure 2.3 Graph showing trends in student results in grief subjects

2017, there were no special interventions for students taking these subjects. In 2018 and 2019, more focused interventions began to be developed for students undertaking these subjects. The graphs show that although there are variations from year to year, there is an emerging trend of decreases in failures and increases in passes and credits. An increase in the number of supps in 2018 may represent some of the decrease in fails converting to near failures and second chances.

Subsequent annual analysis of frequently failed subjects also illustrated how some of the original 11 subjects shifted down the list or fell off it altogether, as staff focused on close monitoring and strategic interventions to support students in these subjects. Improvement in subject results reaffirms the importance of support staff knowing what subjects their students are taking and the degree of risk those subjects imply for their success.

Another area where statistical analysis can draw attention to areas of support that require more attention is students' use of supplementary tutors. Historically, in our current university, there had been a low level of uptake of supplementary tutors by students. Support staff initiated a strategy to increase student use of tutors by allocating tutors at the beginning of semesters to various categories of students deemed to be at risk of failing subjects. What became clear over time is that while tutor usage did increase, not all students were utilising all the hours they were entitled to. This is a persistent issue that is still being worked on. Figure 2.4 illustrates the problem.

The vertical axis indicates the number of tutor hours from 0 to 1600; the horizontal axis plots from left to right the following statistics: the number of students, the number of students who are receiving tutors, the total contract hours the 55 students are entitled to, the tutoring hours that the 55 students actually used, and the number of tutors employed (20). The plot line connecting these illustrates that of the 135 students that one team was responsible for, 55 or less than half had supplementary tutors. This is a pity because this is a funded service available only to Indigenous students, in recognition of their under-preparedness. More worrying and graphically shown in the graph is that out of a total of 1517 hours of tutoring that were available to these 55 students over the semester, only 290 hours were actually utilised. As another team reported in an analysis of their student results, all students who used the full 26 hours of tutoring that they were entitled to over the semester in a subject (2 hours/week) passed those subjects. Failures only occurred among students who did not. Various strategies have been put in place, but it is the reporting of these statistics that keeps reminding support staff that they need to keep checking students are using their tutors and that the relations between students and tutors are working.

Figures 2.5 and 2.6 are graphs that present a statistical analysis of the progress of the full Indigenous student cohort. Figure 2.5 tabulates the raw numbers of annual Indigenous and non-Indigenous completions in our current university

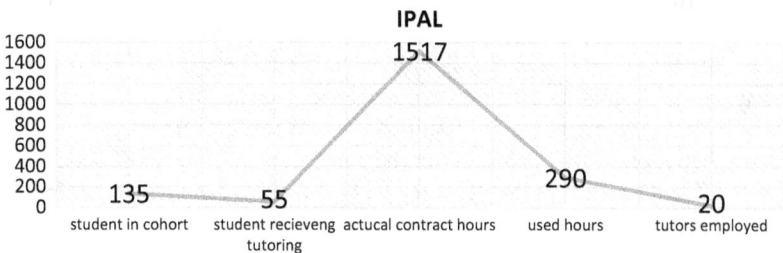

Figure 2.4 Graph showing supplementary tutor usage by students

Completions	2016	2017	2018	2019	2020	2021 (Sem 1)
Indigenous	74	75	106	142	147	51
Non-Indigenous	4544	5176	5440	5315	5780	2331
Total Graduates	4618	5251	5546	5457	5927	2382
Indigenous 5yr Growth		1.4%	42.7%	76.6%	80.2%	
Non-Indigenous 5yr Growth		13.9%	19.0%	16.7%	25.5%	

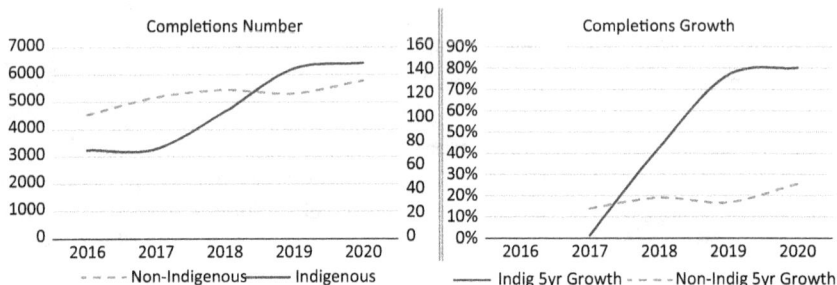

Figure 2.5 Table and graphs of Indigenous student completions and growth of rates of completion compared to non–Indigenous students

from 2016 through to Sem 1, 2021. Below these numbers, it sets out the annual growth in Indigenous and non-Indigenous student completions over the four years from 2017 to 2020. Below this table, these numbers are represented in two graphs. The graph on the left represents the undergraduate completion numbers of both Indigenous and non-Indigenous students from 2016 to 2020. The graph on the right represents the rate of growth of Indigenous completions compared to non-Indigenous students from 2017 to 2020. The purpose of these figures is to underline the impact of changes to the Indigenous student support approach and the efforts of student support managers and staff to improve the effectiveness and efficiency of their services over this period. Non-Indigenous completion rates and growth in the completion rates are expected to be fairly stable because they have not implemented comparable changes. The vertical axis of the lefthand graph indicates the total number of undergraduate students on the left and the number of completions on the right. The horizontal axis indicates left to right the years 2016 to 2020. The broken line represents non-Indigenous students, and the bold line represents Indigenous students. The graph of Indigenous completion numbers reflects the slow beginning of the change process with 74 Indigenous students completing in 2016 and 75 in 2017. However, this was followed by a fairly steep incline to 106 completions in 2018, 142 in 2019, and 147 in 2020. Although it has to be kept in mind that the increases in completions may be attributable to additional factors, such a steep incline is highly likely to be the result of changes to support practices.

If we then look to the graph on the right in Figure 2.5, the vertical axis on the right-hand graph indicates the percentage of growth in completions starting from a base of 0% and rising by ten percentage points until it reaches 90%. The horizontal axis indicates, from left to right, the years 2016 to 2020. The broken line represents non-Indigenous students and the bold line Indigenous students. Once

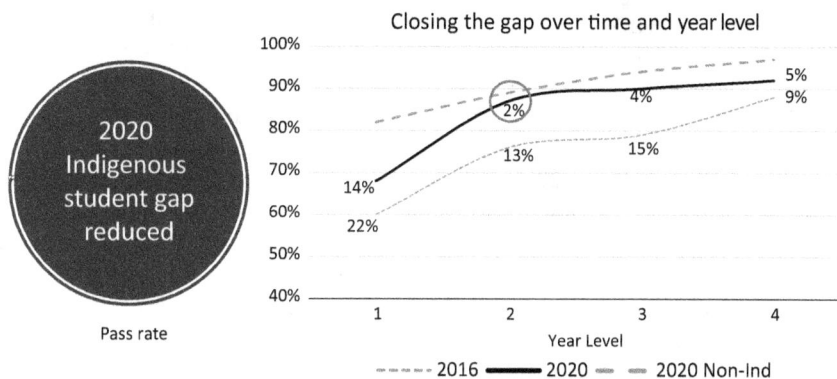

Figure 2.6 Graph showing the closing of the gap between Indigenous and non-Indigenous students' pass rates

again the non-Indigenous students' completion rates, while rising, are relatively stable. However, starting from a base of 0% in 2016, the graph illustrates the steep growth in Indigenous completions from through 2017 and 2018 to 80% followed by a flattening at 80% in 2019 and 2020. Once again, while other factors might be attributed to this growth, the change of approach in student support systems, processes, and practices is certainly implicated in this growth.

Figure 2.6 shows how the gap between Indigenous and non-Indigenous students' subject pass rates has closed since changes to Indigenous student support practices began in 2016. For international readers, 'closing the gap' between Indigenous and non-Indigenous Australians on a range of indicators is a national goal expressed in the Indigenous policy arenas in Commonwealth and State governments. Progress (and lack of progress) in closing the gap is reported annually, including in education. The vertical axis of Figure 2.6 represents subject pass rates in 10% increments from 40% to 100%. The horizontal axis marks the years of undergraduate study from 1st year to 4th year. The dotted graph line represents Indigenous students' subject pass rates for the year 2017. The bold line represents Indigenous students' pass rates for the year 2020. The top broken line represents non-Indigenous students' subject pass rates for 2020. The four sets of percentage points positioned along the Indigenous lines are aligned with each study year level and represent the gap between Indigenous and non-Indigenous pass rates for each of those years of study. The graph shows that the gap between Indigenous and non-Indigenous students' subject pass rates at the end of 1st year was 22% in 2016 and had closed to 14% by 2020. By the 2nd year this gap had closed from 13% in 2016 to 2% in 2020. This suggests that the gap between Indigenous and non-Indigenous students' preparedness at the beginning of the 1st year is probably much greater than 22%. It also affirms what many Indigenous student support staff already know from experience, which is that many Indigenous students require continuing academic and pastoral support beyond the end of the first year. In the 3rd and 4th years, the gap slightly increases to 4% and 5%, respectively, which may reflect the increasing levels of difficulty at those levels and that many Indigenous students are striving to operate independently with only minimal levels of academic learning support.

There are many other ways to make use of local data, for example, an analysis of our student withdrawal statistics indicated a pattern of early withdrawals during the weeks before the census date, followed by a stabilisation during the rest of the semester. This reflects the advice staff give to students about the significance of the census date for incurring fee debts, should they withdraw after that date. Staff awareness of this pattern enabled a discussion about the sorts of efforts made to identify and support struggling students during the first six weeks or whether staff were aware of students' difficulties and reasons for withdrawal. However, this data also prompted a wider discussion at the management and staff level about whether preparation activities, selection criteria, diagnostics and levels of preparation, and inattention to student finances are implicated in causing students to withdraw, causing some reflection on whether these practices need some review or adjustments.

Further, our withdrawal statistics revealed that significant numbers of our students are still struggling to manage learning and/or life during their second year and that an emphasis on early transition and the first-year experience is not enough; it must be extended through the second year to allow students more time to develop the capabilities required to manage the various challenges they encounter. This is particularly useful data for universities with high Indigenous student numbers and low outcomes because attrition and retention rates are one student outcome measurement.

Another analysis explored the outcomes of Indigenous students who were in the university's system but were not studying. This number was equivalent to almost three-quarters of the number of Indigenous students who were actively studying. A special project was established to examine each case and determine such things as where the students were, how far the student had progressed through their studies, how long the student had been away from study and whether the student intended to return to their studies at a later date. Not all students could be contacted. Some had moved to other universities, and some revealed that they were on a break but would be returning. However, the analysis also revealed that some students were very close to completion, in some cases only two subjects short. These students were contacted to encourage their return and establish what their support needs might be. All students who had enough credits to qualify for a diploma in tertiary studies were encouraged to apply to the university and referred to the relevant section. This qualification gives incomplete students some recognition of the knowledge and skills they have gained in university study, which they can use in the job market.

Another use of student data currently being pursued is the monitoring of relations between variables understood to influence student success and GPA levels under and over four. This uses the scales for tracking students' movements towards independence and their capacity levels for academic learning, finance, and wellbeing. While we do not have sufficient data yet to make any major claims about influences on success in our own university, some influences on success are emerging as more significant than others. Finance is unsurprisingly confirmed as a major influence on success, as measured by GPA, as is students' ability to self-regulate their learning. Identification of significant influences will assist staff to identify where to place their support efforts.

Staff knowledge, strategies, skills, and responses to students

Chapter 2 has so far discussed matters that can be considered and some of the components that drive the engine of the monitoring and tracking system. However, to reach its destination, the engine must be driven in the right direction, and it requires an energy source to propel it towards this end. The engine drivers are support staff, and the source of energy is the knowledge, understanding, and commitment of the support staff to assist students. To respond effectively to students' needs, support staff need some understanding of the demands and expectations of higher education learning regarding specific disciplines and courses, what constitutes adequate study conditions, and the administrative rules and regulations about course progressions. Further, staff require knowledge about the various influences on students' academic success and the known impediments to Indigenous students' success. Because of the complex interplay between individual student attributes and circumstances and institutional and external factors, support staff need skills for communicating sensitively, professionally, and effectively with individual students to discover the cause of a student's problem or issue.

Without a sound knowledge base, support staff will rely largely on their experiences or established practices to help students develop the knowledge, skills, and strategies required to succeed in learning and eventually manage with minimal support. Staff develop their knowledge skills and dispositions through experiences with different students and situations and contribute much to students' successes. However, in our experience, not all staff have a thorough understanding of the processes involved in higher education learning or the nature of the efforts required by underprepared learners who have gaps in the knowledge required to understand some of their course content and the technical and strategic skills for learning how to learn in higher education. Further, some staff do not know how important the experience of cumulative successes in academic tasks is for students' belief in their abilities, confidence, and motivation to persist. The narrative about the role that institutional barriers play in Indigenous student outcomes allows some staff to undervalue the importance of students' own efforts, as well as the importance of their own work to support the efforts students must exert to succeed.

We are not suggesting this is a fault of Indigenous student support staff. These frontline workers are instrumental in the success of Indigenous students and have been for decades. However, they are a largely overlooked and neglected workforce. They deserve more opportunities to develop their knowledge and skills and much more understanding of the challenges involved in the work that they do or should do. Professional development is essential to any plan to improve the effectiveness of Indigenous student support, as are more efficient systems and processes for the case management of individual students.

From our experiences working with staff, support staff will likely experience some uncertainty about how students' capacities are to be developed, given the complex interplay of influences on success and the many challenges these produce for underprepared Indigenous students. The support staff will likely be seeking strategies to enable them to help students develop the capabilities they need. However, this book proposes that if they are well informed and possess sufficient relevant knowledge, experience, and regular reflections and reviews, support staff are better placed than academic researchers to devise strategies for assisting students. We suggest that staff will gain more control over their actions and the confidence to change and adjust these actions using the cycle of planning, execution, and review of their approaches and strategies.

Because achieving academic success involves a complex interplay of personal, institutional, and external influences, it is not possible or practical to prescribe specific strategies for staff to follow for different student issues. Therefore, we have included only a few examples while emphasising their limits and the value of developing strategies for the specific context. However, the importance of students learning how to integrate and apply cognitive, metacognitive, motivational, and affective skills in their learning and the complex interplay of influences on student success (see Chapter 1) suggest that an important role of student support staff is to help students become aware of, recognise, and manage the relations between the social, emotional, and academic aspects of their university experiences. This is an important part of students' personal growth and their movement towards becoming more independent and in charge of their learning. Developing students' self-awareness as learners is a central element of a student capacity development approach. This task might seem quite daunting, even unrealistic, for support staff who are not accustomed to working within the bigger picture of the social, emotional, and academic aspects of learning. This is particularly the case where Indigenous student support has operated with a clear division between pastoral and academic support, especially if academic support has relied on supplementary tutors or faculties and has largely been beyond the purview of support staff.

However, helping students develop this self-awareness is not as difficult as staff might imagine. Students often develop this self-awareness as a matter of course, though often very slowly. This awareness can be developed more quickly by helping students talk about what they are doing and how they are going, which can be achieved during student–staff contact points. Even if students do not explicitly talk about their feelings and emotions, these conversations often reveal insights into their emotional states and attributes, such as enthusiasm, shyness, anxiety, frustration, negativity, initiative, passivity, or overconfidence. These insights can help the staff determine how best to understand and respond to a student's issue.

Students' emotional states can also be remembered when assisting students. For example, helping a student with an administrative task such as enrolment always involves more than the technical aspects of the task; it also includes emotional support in the form of reassurance and constructive feedback. Likewise, an academic skill such as 'semester planning' is never just about telling students to plan their time or how to plan. It also involves telling students about the benefits of planning, for example, the emotional and practical benefits of feeling organised, having a plan to keep on top of the workload, developing a sense of control over their tasks, and reducing feelings of panic or being overwhelmed. Conversely, just telling students the benefits of being organised and planning their time will not necessarily deliver those benefits unless they have the skills to plan and organise themselves. Similarly, settling a student who is distressed about other students' opinions in tutorial discussions is not just about affirming their emotional responses but also involves giving students other perspectives and practical ideas for managing these learning situations so that they are not so emotionally affected.

These connections between learning demands and strategic skills for managing the academic and emotional demands of learning provide a logic through which staff can tune their listening skills when talking to students. However, because students do not always make these connections themselves, they are also useful for staff when advising students regarding any academic skill or study behaviour. That is, in a capacity development approach, students benefit from knowing why certain skills and strategies are being advised and how these might help them towards better academic or emotional outcomes and more enjoyable learning and social interactions. Conversations and strategies that help students increase their sense of control over their learning, sense of competency for tasks, learning efficiency, interactions with academics and peers, and sense of belonging and resilience cannot be prescribed; they form part of the personal art of support and this art develops with knowledge of students, the learning process, and the job. Thus, during their conversations with students, staff need to become more attuned to the evidence of students' emotional states, learning challenges, strengths, weaknesses, and levels of capabilities, if they are to assist their development.

Notes

1 See the 'Daily workloads and individual staff task lists' section in this chapter.
2 https://www.willowsoft.com.au/
3 See the section in this chapter on 'Developing student profiles' for information on traffic light systems.
4 See Chapter 1 in this book.
5 For non-Australian readers, the provision of supplementary tutors to provide extra and individual tutoring for Indigenous students is a Commonwealth government-funded scheme, in recognition of past policies that disadvantaged Indigenous people in education.
6 For more information, see http://willowsoft.com.au.

3 Shifting to a capacity development approach

This chapter draws from our experiences of implementing changes in practice in two universities and is primarily intended to be useful for managers and change leaders; however, it also builds a bigger picture for support staff and may help inform the professional development process. Before support managers institute or adjust the systems, processes, and strategies to support the capacity development of Indigenous learners, it helps to consider the main issues implicated in any reform or adjustment process. This includes determining the main aims of Indigenous support services, before exploring what aspects of services and practices might need to be adjusted to support student capacity development goals.

Defining goals for Indigenous student support practices

Academic success

Although what constitutes success for Indigenous higher education students is contested,[1] the overarching goal of our support approach is the *academic success of all* Indigenous students. This is the primary goal for two reasons. First, most Indigenous students enter university with an aspiration to complete their preferred degrees and they accrue considerable debt to do so. Second, the purpose of Indigenous student support provisions in Australian universities is to support students to reach their academic goals.

From the student support perspective, academic success means passing subjects and completing courses with as few subject repeats as possible and as promptly as possible, taking into consideration a student's particular personal circumstances.[2] In certain situations, these circumstances may cause some students to defer their studies, reduce their study loads, or decide that university is not their best option. While the role of support staff is to provide advice to help students make the best decision in these cases, the support staff also have the responsibility of doing all they can to ensure a student in difficult circumstances can continue with their studies and, if possible, maintain their subject load. Our experience is that care needs to be taken when giving routine advice to students who experience challenges or setbacks to decrease their subject loads. When giving this advice, it is critical to be mindful of the intersections between ADSTUDY, scholarships, and other financial assistance criteria and study loads, and the effects of the extended time a student

DOI: 10.4324/9781003326458-4

will have to study to complete their course. Students should always be offered guidance, support, and strategies first for managing difficult circumstances.

From the support perspective, academic progress refers to students' progression through their courses towards completion. Students who continually fail subjects each semester or switch between courses over the years cannot be considered to be making good progress. They are also accumulating debts and extending their study duration considerably. Therefore, academic progress also depends on students passing rather than failing subjects.

Achieving improvements in students' learning outcomes also means helping students achieve academic standards that reflect their abilities and potential. Credits and above-GPAs are a useful benchmark for staff when supporting the incremental development of students' capacities. Most Indigenous students can achieve these standards if given the right support to strengthen their confidence, self-belief in their capabilities, and motivation to complete their studies and develop the skills and strategies they need. Although there will always be some students who will not reach these achievement standards or their full potential, the academic success goal reminds staff about the importance of their role in student outcomes and provides a target they can work towards. Working towards a clear academic goal places the emphasis on staff to constantly reflect on the effectiveness of their work.

As the overarching goal, academic success does not diminish the purpose of or need for pastoral (personal, social, or cultural) support. On the contrary, it renews attention to the significance of pastoral support for students' academic successes and the role that adequate finances, suitable and affordable accommodation, social support, life–work–study balance, and socio-emotional wellbeing have in a student's ability to stay in their studies and succeed academically. The discussions of key educational concepts and study conditions in Chapter 1 indicate this. Both academic and pastoral support strategies and interventions are integral to Indigenous students' academic success. Because the interplay or connections between personal challenges and academic ones are implicated in students' chances of success, there is a case for strengthening the links between academic and pastoral staff roles and the information exchanges that need to occur between them.

Developing the capabilities of independent learners

This goal is more refined and recognises that higher education learning is premised on the expectation that students are responsible for their own efforts, expected to be reasonably independent in how they conduct their learning, and if they are experiencing difficulties, expected to self-initiate requests for advice or assistance. In the context of Indigenous students' relative under-preparedness, the task of student support staff is to support students in their efforts to determine what they have to do to achieve success in academic tasks and help them develop the capabilities— knowledge, skills, and strategies—they need to do so. However, when facilitating this goal, support staff also need to be mindful of the need for students to eventually manage the demands and challenges of academic learning on their own, with minimal levels of support. This implies that while students need support in the form of guidance and assistance, support is best provided in a way that enables students to develop the capabilities they need to eventually feel in control and take charge of their own learning. This development does not occur evenly over time but varies considerably among students, subjects, and disciplines. Nevertheless, the overall trend should be a movement towards increased independence.

As our discussions of the key concepts in Chapter 1 revealed, the capabilities of successful and relatively independent learners are not confined to academic learning but extend to managing other aspects of their life circumstances that affect their chances of academic success. This suggests that academic and pastoral support are integral to student success and that there is a case for reconsidering how these roles are synchronised to support students.

Minimal support can be interpreted as the occasional support that relatively independent students might require from Indigenous support staff to overcome challenges that they are unable to successfully resolve on their own. Other sources of support these students may routinely use include consulting and learning from friends, peers, course tutors, academics, librarians, university services, counsellors, or others in their lives who are in a position to offer guidance or advice. However, it must be remembered that specialised Indigenous student support provisions exist because other avenues of support across the university often present additional challenges for Indigenous students. This is especially the case for underprepared and unconfident students but also relatively independent students, in situations where cultural and personal sensitivities or race are involved. Discomfort in classrooms, difficulties connecting with student peers, nervousness or shame about approaching lecturers or course tutors for assistance (or the time it takes for academics and course tutors to respond to their queries), the presence of fewer significant others who understand their challenges at university and who can give them useful advice, and a reluctance to engage with standard university services are common situations for Indigenous students. Students who are confident enough to use these services should be encouraged but not forced to do so.

As students become more independent, some who have developed the necessary capabilities and confidence will move away from IEUs or Indigenous student support staff; others just as capable will continue to make the IEU their home base for social and cultural support. However, the progress of all relatively independent students still needs to be monitored. This extends to high-achieving students who gain direct entry to university and/or can manage without specialised assistance from commencement. The underperformance of capable and relatively independent students should always be investigated, and support should be offered.

In the support process, the developmental goal is pivoted towards developing the capabilities students need to manage challenges as they arise as the key to building students' self-confidence and belief in their own abilities. Part of managing on their own will include the confidence to continue asking for help whenever a challenge, academic or personal, threatens their success or ability to continue studying. During this process, students are developing lifelong learning skills they will need throughout their careers and an important general life skill that will serve them well in other areas of their lives.

When introducing these two goals to staff, it is essential that managers provide them with background knowledge about the concepts of university readiness/

under-preparation and independent learners/learning. This constitutes the initial professional development stage associated with the change process.

Finding a frame for the student support approach

When considering how to implement a capacity development approach to student support provisions and services, it is useful to review whether the current framing of the student support approach is aligned with the two goals and whether the current framework enables or impedes the support provisions and practices needed to achieve those goals. However, what is meant by framing? Think of a picture frame or a window frame. A frame focuses attention on certain things and takes attention away from things outside the frame. In the context of Indigenous student support, a frame directs staff attention to particular ways of understanding, considering, and discussing students, their issues, and their support needs. That is, a frame helps direct the way staff perceive, understand, interpret, and respond to student situations. How an approach to student support is framed can reflect and shape the thinking and practices of staff. Thus, a frame also helps establish or reflect the agenda for student support—an agenda revealed in the goals, organisation, priorities, and practices of student support services and the attitudes, dispositions, and actions of staff towards students and their needs.

Frames are generally not made explicit, and therefore, staff can be quite unaware of what the main frame is for the way they understand, interpret, and respond to student issues. Further, staff can be unaware of the things they are not thinking or talking about. Becoming aware of framing assists staff in recognising some of the implicit frames that may shape their own services and responses to students' needs and situations. To make this a little clearer, the subsequent sections briefly describe some framing examples that may apply to Indigenous student support approaches currently in use in different universities. Our view is that none of these is sufficient as a primary frame for student support, even though the issues they address are relevant to students' needs.

Deficit-based frames

Deficit-based frames construct Indigenous students as deficient and blame or judge Indigenous students or their families for their life predicaments and their under-preparation for higher education. A deficit-based frame conveniently forgets the social determinants and institutional practices that contribute to and perpetuate Indigenous people's relative socio-economic and educational disadvantage. When applied to student support services, deficit-based frames are counterproductive to a student's progress and success agenda: 'discourses that blame individuals tend to exacerbate feelings of incapability in both teachers and students.'[3]

However, acknowledging that Indigenous students have some deficits in the knowledge, skills, and resources they need to succeed is not necessarily to be operating from within a deficit-based frame, as long as these deficits are not equated to students' inherent abilities or characterised as their own fault. Rather, students' under-preparedness for university should position the student support agenda (and the rest of the university) as one that *bears a responsibility to help* under-prepared Indigenous students develop the knowledge, skills, resources, and capabilities they need to function successfully in their learning.

Further, there is more to avoiding deficit-based frames of Indigenous students than just calling out negatively perceived institutional practices or discourses. Indigenous student support practices and discourses must also be examined for hidden assumptions and deficit-based judgements about individual students, which can lead to some students being overlooked or screened out of student support provisions to which they are entitled. The way staff understand, discuss, and make assumptions about Indigenous students' backgrounds, identities, and capabilities must be open for examination and reflection for evidence of any deficit positioning of students, as do staff attitudes and dispositions towards assisting students.

Crisis management frames

Crisis management frames are commonly developed by governments and other organisations who need to understand the risks, threats, and vulnerabilities of populations to potential crises to respond effectively. No Indigenous student support centre would view their current approach as one framed primarily by crisis management practices. However, we have observed approaches to Indigenous student support that are very close to this framing.

One of the aims of any student support approach should be to avoid students reaching crisis points that threaten their chances of success or continuing their studies. If staff *predominantly* have contact with students for the first time when they are already experiencing serious difficulties, at risk of failing or exclusion, or when their socio-emotional wellbeing is at a crisis point, they have not developed adequate support strategies and are predominantly operating as a crisis management service. Nevertheless, Indigenous student support staff need processes and procedures for managing students experiencing crises because there will always be students who experience crises that they cannot manage independently. However, crisis management should never be the main frame of student support practices.

Remedial frames

Remedial approaches focus on 'catching up' students in specific subject content and skills they require for their courses. The issue with understanding student support as largely a remediation exercise is that this framing does not adequately recognise the complex interplay of many other factors that affect students' chances of success, including student, institutional, and external factors. However, it is important to consider the context in which remediation occurs and how it fits into the overall student support approach. For example, in the Indigenous student support context, there is an indicated need to focus on the gaps in students' core knowledge and skills assumed by their courses. Therefore, remediation work is a legitimate and necessary form of assistance.

However, as the main frame for the support approach, a remedial frame risks primarily perceiving students narrowly in terms of their knowledge and skill deficits rather than in the broader terms of their strengths, potential, and other attributes. Consequently, the complex interplay of influences and different sets of knowledge, skills, and behavioural strategies that are also integral to students' outcomes receive less attention. Some of these will have a critical role in the progress or withdrawal of underprepared students. Chapter 1 explored these key concepts and stressed the importance of students' integration of skills and strategies and management of negative influences in their learning approaches. Therefore, remedial frames are insufficient for Indigenous student support, although effective student support will include remedial work with many Indigenous students. Much of that work can be done by supplementary tutors.

Advocacy frames

An advocacy approach to student support is one where support staff primarily understand their role as being an advocate for the student, as a way to mediate between the institution and the student. This has been an established practice in many IEUs because, until recently, Indigenous support staff were often compelled to adopt the role of advocates to make a case for adjustments to practices in other areas of the university in the interests of Indigenous students. Now that Indigenous people occupy senior positions and can drive Indigenous strategies across their university, the lines between Indigenous support staff advocacy for students and Indigenous advocacy for wider institutional changes, including changes in the interests of students, are more clearly delineated. This gives more time and space for student support staff to focus on their own practices and whether they aid student efforts.

In the light of these changes, advocacy, as a routine response to students' challenges or setbacks, does not adequately serve student success and capacity development. Routine advocacy has the potential to undermine the agency of students and bypass the support task of assisting students to develop the capabilities they need to become more independent managers of their learning. Part of the student effort involves developing the capabilities needed to act in an agentive, purposeful way to mediate the effects of negative influences and setbacks through their own actions. In a capacity development approach, the primary role of staff is to support the students' efforts by assisting students to develop the knowledge, strategies, and skills that will help them overcome challenges and setbacks.

Advocacy as a routine support response can also distract staff from investigating the sources of students' challenges, including students' own actions and behaviours, which may contribute to or prevent them from accurately assessing the causes of their difficulties. Indigenous student support managers and staff should never ask academics to pass students because of their own mismanagement of students. No Indigenous student is entitled to a pass if they have not met the standards, nor are their future interests well-served by such advocacy.

Therefore, as a frame, advocacy is also insufficient for supporting the needs of students. Nevertheless, there will always be some student situations where advocacy or interventions by support staff on behalf of students will be appropriate. These support staff interventions are generally those needed to secure a better outcome for an individual student, for example, an assessment extension, a re-marking for an assessment, an adjustment of exam conditions, or exceptions to course progression rules in exceptional circumstances. Advocacy may also be an appropriate intervention when a student requires financial or emergency assistance, other special considerations, and, in some cases, apologies (and longer-term remedies) for racist treatment. However, before advocating for individual students, consideration needs to be given to whether sufficient support has been extended to a student and whether the interventions sought by staff are warranted and in the student's best interests. In some cases, staff advocacy will be warranted; in others, it will not be. In most cases, if students are given effective assistance in the form of relevant information and language, they will be able to advocate for special considerations themselves and, if not, should be assisted to do so. This is part of taking charge of their learning and aids feelings of control over negative circumstances.

Indigenous cultural frames

Consistent with the national policy, the Indigenous higher education sector is committed to the relevance and importance of Indigenous perspectives and cultural issues in higher education.[4] This commitment extends to support practices. IEUs are culturally framed to the extent that they are Indigenous spaces that are staffed by mostly Indigenous staff who use culturally familiar social and communicative ways of relating to students. They offer students a place of refuge from the stress of engaging in the wider university and social support from Indigenous staff and fellow students in culturally familiar forms and, in many places, from community Elders. Many IEUs also act as the centre of cultural activities in the university.

However, the position of Aboriginal and Torres Strait Islander culture in Indigenous students' higher education and its relation to student learning success is a complex issue. It carries different kinds and levels of meaning, relevance, and importance for different students, depending on their cultural backgrounds, courses of study, and career goals. In the context of student support, the cultural backgrounds and identities of students are significant because these can affect their sense of belonging, expectations regarding the treatment and inclusion of Indigenous content in academic courses, confidence to engage in teaching/learning contexts, and moods and emotions. Challenges with regard to any of these areas can then affect engagement, motivation, learning, and wellbeing. Further, some students (e.g., those from rural and remote areas, studying away from home, and first-in-family students) are often distanced from their usual social and cultural supports and have an increased risk of feeling isolated or uncomfortable in the university environment. A cultural framing also supports the inclusion of Indigenous values in the support culture and staff practices. As a best practice, this engenders a sense of belonging or community that can boost students' confidence to engage with learning and others in the wider university community. As a worst practice, this can support unprofessional practices that favour some Indigenous students over others.

Despite the positive benefits of cultural frames, they should never seek to confine students to their comfort zone. Care should be taken that the cultural frame is not limited to a cultural safety frame, even though that is one of its important functions. Rather, the cultural frame should also pivot staff towards equipping students to be confident in their Indigenous identities in non-Indigenous spaces and with their non-Indigenous peers. Helping students achieve successful outcomes and feel as competent as their non-Indigenous peers is critical to their confidence, as the discussions regarding self-efficacy, self-regulated learning, motivation, and persistence in Chapter 1 made clear.[5]

Additionally, it helps to remember that higher education is a transformative process that will stretch students in various ways, which can be an unsettling experience. All students experience difficult and uncomfortable situations, and with assistance, Indigenous students can develop strategies to recognise and manage these feelings. When students experience discomfort and distress directly related to their Indigenous status, the role of support in a capacity development approach is to provide students with strategies that enable them to better manage during and after these situations. In some situations where students' university experiences trigger trauma or more profound setbacks, it is necessary to talk to faculty staff and others higher up and suggest and help students to access appropriate professional sources of assistance. This applies to racist or other difficult encounters with university staff and students, which is a whole-of-university concern and responsibility to address. Patterns of discomfort and distress related to particular cohorts, subjects, courses, or environments are also issues for staff to refer to managers for discussions at faculty levels and with Indigenous senior staff responsible for the whole-of-university strategy.

Generally speaking, while IEUs are important spaces for students to find support and while they can be thought of as a refuge or home away from home, the staff's role is also to assist students in developing their strengths and attributes so they can be independent outside the IEU and their own community. A sign of successful student support is students who grow to be comfortable with their non-Indigenous peers, able to interact well with academics and tutors, at home in their faculties and university environments, and able to defend their sense of self, either assertively or psychologically, using language and communication or mental processing and self-messaging strategies.

A positive cultural framing that prioritises students' academic success is beneficial and valuable for Indigenous students if it is non-judgemental of their varying identity journeys, community networks, family histories, knowledge and experiences of Indigenous knowledge, languages and cultures, and future career goals. In our experience, creating a positive, inclusive, and professional support culture encourages the diversity of Indigenous students to participate in the cultural life of the IEU and learn from one another's experiences of being Indigenous.

The benefits of a cultural frame are acknowledged as an essential part of the student support effort. However, a cultural frame is insufficient to help students develop all the necessary capacities to succeed in a university. The cultural frame needs to work alongside and support an educational framing of student support practices.

Strengths-based frames

Strengths-based educational approaches recognise that individuals have their own strengths, goals, attributes, personal resources, and potential that can be developed.

In strengths-based education, the problems or challenges facing individuals are considered the result of individuals' circumstances and positions rather than deficits within the individuals. Strengths-based approaches do not deny that students have problems and challenges, but the focus on strengths offers a different language or narrative for discussing challenges, one that enables a more positive expectation that students' capabilities can be developed. Therefore, the language of strengths-based educational practices is future-oriented, non-judgemental, and raises students' awareness of their potential. This awareness has been linked to students' choices and decisions concerning engagement, applying their strengths when approaching tasks, and their future career directions.[6]

While there is a strong expectation that individuals can change their ways of doing things, develop their knowledge, skills, and inner resources, and progress towards their desired goals, simply focusing on and affirming students' positive strengths is insufficient and does little to help a student to keep building the extended capabilities they need. Thus, in any strengths-based approach, there must also be an emphasis on the importance of student efforts in the developmental process and the time and practice involved when learning new knowledge, strategies, and skills.[7]

Research on strengths-based education draws on insights from education, psychology, social work, and organisational theory and behaviour and is commonly applied in social work and other human services where case management approaches are used.[8] Strengths-based approaches have been criticised for placing too much responsibility on individuals and neglecting the role of wider social and institutional determinants.[9] Therefore, a strengths-based approach to Indigenous student support should be balanced by ensuring that systemic social and institutional determinants are being addressed by others in the university and through advice to government agencies and policymakers.

We also suggest that any strengths-based approach should ensure that Indigenous students' strengths are properly recognised by support staff as assets contributing to their success. This suggests that understandings of Indigenous students' social and personal strengths need to be academically contextualised, for example, the value of Indigenous peer cooperation and social support networks for learning, or the value of some Indigenous students' oral and communicative skills for academic presentations as strengths that can be supplemented by assisting them with the academic substance of their presentations, or the value of determination and commitment as strengths that can be extended to develop a student's control over learning, written communication skills or persistence and resilience. Indigenous students' cultural strengths should also be academically contextualised so that, for example, students' Indigenous knowledge, experiences, or perspectives are recognised as assets that can be harnessed to develop their understanding of the value and limits of disciplinary knowledge.

The frames discussed in this section are not the only available frameworks. There are other ways to frame student support services that might shape or reflect how support staff understand their roles and practices regarding students, for example, equity, social inclusion, Indigenous rights, or therapeutic frames, which might be evident in some contexts. Considering the predominant current frames may enable managers and staff to think more about the strengths and limits of their current practices, for example: What are they focused on? What do they not pay attention to or consider in the way they deliver support services?

Aligning the support frame with goals: A capacity development frame

The previous section in this chapter illustrated how particular frames have a role in shaping or reflecting approaches to student support practices.[10] This section describes a frame through which staff can begin to shape the support services towards the two identified goals: academic success and developing independent learners.[11] We have called this a student capacity development frame, and it has helped shape an agenda for reforming and developing support practices. The development of this frame has been informed by research and the student support reforms we have led in two universities. The subsequent change agenda has been implemented in practice over time.

In some university contexts, other goals and frames may serve the needs of student cohorts and help support staff shape their practices in the desired direction. Our only caution is that those choices and decisions must be informed by sound research and auditing of current practices and analyses of student outcomes. This section provides the main reference points in an individual student capacity development frame for Indigenous student support.

A *student capacity development frame* incorporates a *strengths-based approach* because it recognises and builds on students' strengths and takes a developmental approach to further building student capacities according to individuals' indicated needs. Further, it incorporates a secondary *cultural framing* that is future-oriented and non-judgemental. The *cultural framing* also focuses staff towards an awareness of cultural issues that may emerge in individual students' management of their learning and personal circumstances and operationalises a cultural ethic of care for all students based on an Indigenous family model. This family model expresses the idea that students and staff belong to one interconnected family, with staff looking out for all students and students looking out for each other and respecting staff. The ethic of care requires staff to know their students and keep abreast of their needs for assistance.

Therefore, a student capacity development frame rejects the deficit, remedial, crisis management, and advocacy frames as suitable primary frames.[12] Nevertheless, a student capacity development frame acknowledges that many students will have knowledge and skill deficits and that for many students, this will indicate the need for remedial work. A student capacity development frame also recognises that, sometimes, staff will be assisting students experiencing crises and will also be required to advocate on behalf of students. This implies that staff should be responsive to students' needs without limiting how they understand and respond to them to develop the required capacities to succeed.

A student capacity development frame also repositions the cultural frame to a secondary support position and refocuses it towards helping students develop the capacities to become successful independent learners with skills and strategies to manage in their future professions, without leaving their Indigenous identities behind. In this approach, support staff view students' Indigenous identities, knowledge, and experiences as attributes that can lead them to a deeper understanding of their positions in the world when dealing with misrepresentations or omissions of Indigenous realities in the academic disciplines. Therefore, a capacity development frame pivots cultural support towards helping students develop strategies to manage and grow from uncomfortable learning and social situations, in preparation for their future professional lives. Simultaneously, a capacity development approach recognises that some Indigenous students will suffer emotionally and psychologically from incidents in universities' teaching and learning, administrative, and social environments and that an important role of support staff is to support and guide all students in such situations and defend and intervene on their behalf when warranted.

In terms of staff practice, an Indigenous student capacity development frame shapes staff roles and responsibilities towards knowing the educational starting points and personal attributes and circumstances of the students they are responsible for; respecting the strengths of their students and not judging their predicaments; understanding students' challenges and the possible contributing influences that enable or impede successful outcomes; and understanding the knowledge, skills, attributes, and capabilities students need to achieve successful outcomes. It also involves developing strategies, dispositions, and language to determine individual students' support needs; developing strategies and processes to support students' efforts at developing the capabilities they need to learn with minimal support; having a process for monitoring and tracking student progress towards the two goals (i.e., academic success and independence as learners); and having a process for reviewing and evaluating areas of their work that might require adjustments to be more effective.

The transition to a student capacity development frame is likely to be difficult for many staff in the practical sense. This is especially the case in situations where Indigenous student support narratives and practices have centred on advocacy for students, crisis management, or therapeutic approaches to students' challenges that prioritise cultural affirmation rather than assisting students to navigate the tensions between their Indigenous and emerging student/learner/future professional identities. Part of the role of managers during any change process will be managing these older narratives to keep them in perspective in the minds and practices of staff.

The following sections discuss the elements of a student capacity development frame to illustrate the aspects of current services and practices that might be reexamined and tweaked to reshape the broad direction of student support provisions, strategies, and practices. These are areas for managers to consider when auditing current practices and in the planning process, whatever the reform intentions might be.

The whole-of-education journey

The whole-of-education journey refers to students' journeys from school or community through to graduation and postgraduate studies. Each university organises interventions, activities, and strategies for Indigenous students along this journey according to the broader Indigenous strategy within the university, the perceived needs of students, and the available resources or expertise. Whole-of-education journey activities usually fall into three spheres of activity: pre-entry, selection-for-entry, and post-entry strategies. Pre-entry activities are designed to encourage prospective students to access higher education. These activities aim to build the pipeline of students into higher education and increase their chances of access. They form part of the university marketing and student recruitment exercise; however, educationally, they should give students a realistic measure of whether university is appropriate for them and provide them with enough information, experience, and guidance to make good decisions and choices. Selection-for-entry programs are designed to provide alternative or supplementary selection criteria that consider more than prior educational attainment for enrolment offers and entry decisions. Post-entry strategies are designed to keep enrolled enabling, undergraduate, and postgraduate coursework students in the pipeline until they complete their studies.[13]

Under a student capacity development frame, the explicit goal for activities at all stages should be to increase students' chances of success in their studies by taking every opportunity to develop participants' knowledge regarding how the university works, realistic expectations of the efforts that higher education study requires, and the requisites, capacities, and study conditions students will need to have the best chances of success, and raise awareness of the availability and benefits of support designed to assist them. These opportunities to develop prospective students' knowledge apply to outreach and aspiration-building activities for school students, which should strive to include actual learning experiences in areas of student interest. Pre-entry and aspiration-building activities use many resources and should not shield Indigenous participants from the educational reality of higher education. We suggest that any review of the approach to student support needs to consider the alignment of activities and programs along this journey and review the activities/strategies themselves.

When considering any changes or adjustments, student support managers should also decide what stages of the journey to prioritise in the immediate to longer terms. Decisions about priorities will likely vary according to the specific contexts of different universities. For example, some universities with retention, success, and completion rates approaching those of other Australian students but with low numbers of Indigenous students may want to prioritise increasing those numbers, which might involve improving their pathway programs and alignments. Those with high numbers and low outcomes may want to prioritise improving support practices for enrolled students. In other universities, a review might reveal that some simultaneous adjustments of programs and activities in all stages are appropriate and manageable. In all situations, reviews will likely indicate that some level of change is required for all three stages and that the extent and urgency of the work in any area might determine where to begin and what the priorities should be.

Any changes that involve negotiations with others in or outside the university are likely to take time and effort on the part of managers and may require higher-level discussions to facilitate changes. Examples of these intersections include changes to pre-entry activities that require in-kind or financial contributions from the faculties or university, changes to selection-for-entry processes and decisions involving faculty and Indigenous staff, changes to university-run tertiary preparation programs that are failing to meet Indigenous needs, initiatives for pathway programs involving other providers within or outside the university, issues associated with student financial assistance (e.g., negotiating the criteria for scholarship eligibilities and the timing of income distribution), expanding residential accommodation for Indigenous students, allocating Higher Education Participation and Partnerships Program funds, and improving alignments between Indigenous outreach and recruitment and university marketing and recruitment programs.

Changes to activities and support practices in all areas are likely to involve the professional development of staff, which requires time and effort to plan. As part of the review process and to plan priorities for change, we have found it useful to work backwards. First, this requires a sound understanding of what enrolled students need to do to succeed in both enabling and undergraduate programs. Second, a review of the selection-for-entry process is required to determine whether the selection criteria, processes, and decisions are adequate for identifying a student who has a reasonable chance of succeeding in enabling and undergraduate courses if they are given the right support. Third, a review of pre-entry activities will help determine how much these contribute towards preparing students for the demands of Indigenous enabling programs, university preparation programs, or undergraduate courses. Priorities for adjustments and changes can be established based on these three audit measures and an analysis of the current outcomes of Indigenous students who have journeyed through these activities or programs.

In our reforms in two universities, we initially prioritised improving the support for enrolled students. Enrolled students are already in the pipeline, at risk of accruing financial debts, and have been given entry on the expectation that they can succeed. For those universities with low retention, success, and completion rates, attending to the needs of all students already in the pipeline helps improve these rates. Prioritising improvements to access rates in the context of a university's low success and completion rates risks ongoing low success and completion rates. Thus, especially in the context of low student outcomes, support for enrolled students is an indicated priority for changes. However, this does not suggest that our approach to reform does not provide for simultaneous efforts to review and improve alternative selection processes and to review and adjust preparation programs and pre-entry activities. Rather, it suggests that reviews/audits and changes in those areas did not take precedence over improving support for all enrolled students.

Access pathways, pre-entry, and tertiary preparation programs

Access pathways, Indigenous pre-entry enabling programs, and university tertiary preparation programs aim to improve the readiness of Indigenous students to succeed in degree programs. Access and enabling programs provide an educational pipeline into degree programs. They continue to be critical to the success of many Indigenous higher education students, and without them, the number of Indigenous graduates would be significantly lower.[14] Ideally, Indigenous pathways programs, Indigenous pre-program activities, and university preparation programs should complement each other or align sufficiently to enable students to increase their capacity development incrementally along their educational journey and achieve a growing sense of control and incremental academic successes in the process. While there are some good examples of Indigenous pathways programs in the literature, there is less research regarding the efficacy of access, pathways, and enabling programs.[15]

Thus, despite the benefits of these programs for Indigenous students, it is a mistake for managers and support staff to assume that pathways and enabling programs provide the necessary scaffolding for knowledge and skills development to prepare Indigenous students for success in degree programs. It is also a mistake to assume that university tertiary preparation programs provide sufficient preparation for the step-up to degree programs. Therefore, Indigenous student support services have a critical role in ensuring that students in these programs receive the additional support they need. University-wide Indigenous strategies also have a role in reviewing and determining Indigenous needs in this area.

As part of any local review of student support provisions in the pathways and enabling area, there is value in auditing the contents and student outcomes of pathways and preparation programs to discover how they meet Indigenous needs, for example: What do they expect of underprepared Indigenous students? How and what sort of student capacities do they build? How well staged are the incremental steps of capacity building through articulated pathways where these exist? It is also useful to collect local data on withdrawal and subject failure rates to determine specific areas where changes to enabling and preparation programs may be necessary. Audits in this area should include input from someone with a background in education and a sound understanding of Indigenous students' educational starting points and challenges. If this is not possible, we suggest audits involving suitably qualified people with knowledge in these areas.

Such an exercise in one institution highlighted that the tertiary access course (a taster course) and the university tertiary preparation course, both open access, had the highest rates of subject failures of any courses or subjects undertaken by Indigenous students. Part of the explanation for this is that these courses contain a relatively small number of subjects, while Indigenous students in degree programs study thousands of subjects. However, another part of the explanation relates to open access and that the step-ups are too high for many students using these programs as pathways into undergraduate courses. Nevertheless, the actual statistics were confronting, even though staff knew there were high failure and withdrawal rates. If, as the research suggests, students' self-efficacy beliefs depend on feelings of competency and the experience of success, and if competency levels are linked to students' persistence, motivation, engagement, and sense of belonging, then high failure and withdrawal rates may imply that programs are missing the mark.

Similarly, in the same university, an audit of the many possible Technical and Further Education college (TAFE) articulations into the university health enabling programs revealed a large step-up between accepted certificate levels and university preparation courses and undergraduate degree subjects. This gap impedes many Indigenous community workers' chances of higher education success, especially in the health and social work sciences, where there is a strong community need for Indigenous professionals.

In another example from our previous university, an audit of the type of mathematics required by Indigenous students in different disciplines confirmed what seems to be a common problem with university math preparation programs. In most cases, these are condensed versions of years 11–12 math subjects. Although Indigenous students often have significant gaps in their math skills, the math that Indigenous students require varies significantly across different disciplines and courses. Students needing math skills in some disciplines do not require such comprehensive math knowledge as, for example, an engineering student. The math that a social work or psychology student will require is narrower; this is similar for students in the health sciences, business, and primary education disciplines. This suggests that students in university preparation programs could be given more focused assistance in the areas required rather than a full year 12 math curriculum. Curriculum issues are not within the control of Indigenous student support staff, although it is important to raise these issues with relevant program managers and faculties. However, in both these universities, information that the support staff gained from the audit of math programs and students' needs in different disciplines was used to ensure that the staff closely tracked and supported commencing students in enabling degree program math subjects and other degree subjects that included math components. This positively influenced the students' outcomes.

The problems that are uncovered during audits of pathways and enabling alignments indicate the required feedback for those who run tertiary enabling programs and support Indigenous students in faculties or IEUs. However, it is a long-term project to address these sorts of mismatches between enabling subjects and individual or cohort needs, and it is likely that in some universities, it will be difficult for such programs to meet such diverse student needs.

Nevertheless, from the support perspective and in the immediate term, an auditing process is invaluable for determining how best to supplement support for a student where these mismatches occur. Support staff can carry out basic student support tasks, including understanding what a subject or course expects from a student, understanding a student's knowledge and skill gaps and their needs, ensuring students understand the degree of effort required, ensuring students are matched with an appropriate supplementary tutor from the commencement of the semester, and monitoring student progress closely.

However, it should not be overlooked that there will be some Indigenous students on pathways from work to degree programs who may have prior educational attainments or sufficient attributes, skills, and capacities to go directly into degree programs. These prospective students will require some form of diagnostic assessments during the selection-for-entry to avoid too liberal an interpretation of recognising their prior learning, which can and does set up students to fail.

Selection-for-entry processes

Alternative selection-for-entry processes provide an important opportunity for reviews in any capacity development approach. A capacity development approach should emphasise selection processes that:

1   identify prospective students who may be set up to fail if given entry due to too large a gap in knowledge, skills, or finance/study conditions; provide such students with further guidance about how to increase their chances of entry in a subsequent year

2   determine entry to enabling and degree programs for underprepared students by considering their prior educational attainments and experiences relevant to their preferred course and the strength of their personal attributes for positively influencing their chances of success

3   make early determinations, in broad terms, about the level of support individual students are likely to need.

Making such determinations presupposes some form of diagnostics to establish applicants' levels of writing, comprehension, and numeracy skills. Diagnostics are particularly indicated for non-school leavers, those who have not completed secondary school or have no year 12 attainment, those with no tertiary ranking scores or those with tertiary ranking scores that are significantly lower than the course cut-off points. We have used adapted post-entry language assessment tasks—commonly known as PELA—developed in collaboration with an expert and to provide key staff with professional development to assess and moderate student assessments. These are basic but well-designed literacy, comprehension, writing, and numeracy assessments that provide insights into students' literacy and numeracy abilities, which helps to gauge the levels of academic readiness/under-preparation of prospective students who have no or low tertiary ranking scores.

Interviews are an equally important part of alternative entry programs. In a student capacity development approach, the interview process should focus on eliciting information that indicates the students' personal attributes, which have a major role in their chances of succeeding, for example, eliciting information about a student's interests and goals, level and sources of motivation, attitudes towards learning, effort and commitment, maturity level, confidence and self-initiative, and self-awareness of their strengths and weaknesses. Interviews are not just for making entry decisions; they also help establish relationships with students and determine their need for financial, accommodation, personal wellbeing, and cultural support.

On their own, interviews are insufficient to gauge a student's academic level, and basic literacy and numeracy diagnostic tests are inadequate for determining the attributes of students that can positively influence their chances of succeeding. The two work best when combined. Students who are not offered entry can always benefit from guidance about what to focus on to increase their readiness for higher education and options in TAFE or other provider institutions.

As an anecdote, we refer to the results of incorporating an adjusted post-entry language assessment diagnostic test alongside the interview process for the first time in a selection-for-entry process in our previous university. From an analysis of the results, staff categorised students according to three levels of risk and need for support: (1) those who would likely require intensive, consistent academic support; (2) those who would likely require regular but less intensive academic support; and (3) those who would likely manage with occasional or minimal assistance.

Newly appointed academic support staff then monitored, maintained contact with, and supported students accordingly. At the end of the year, those in the highest risk group outperformed many of those in the other two groups. This convinced staff of the value of closely monitoring and tracking students and providing effective, timely support to meet individual students' needs. Academic support included increasing the allocation of supplementary tutors as early as possible in the semester and prioritising students in the highest risk category. Before this, academic support had consisted of a part-time, in-house academic tutor and supplementary tutors for those students who requested them.

Intensive preparation programs for particular disciplines can also serve as selection-for-entry programs. These programs expose students to intensive learning and testing and place their personal attributes, strengths, and responses under the scrutiny of the faculty academics who will teach them and the Indigenous staff who will support them. Although there can be different models, these programs are usually residential, conducted over a few weeks, and can be costly to run. They require sponsorship at a level that is particularly hard to find in some universities and extra time from faculty academics during a busy time of the year. Their advantage is the level of confidence and familiarity they build in students in relation to the nature of and effort involved in higher education learning.

In situations where relevant faculty staff conduct the final selections for particular courses, an important role for Indigenous support staff is to gather their own diagnostic and personal attribute information as part of the process. This helps establish the level of support students are likely to need and begin the planning required to support students from day one.

Communicating with prospective students via the tertiary admissions centre application processes is another avenue for understanding prospective students and whether their educational backgrounds or expected results are likely to match their course interests and requirements. Establishing relationships with prospective students at this stage provides opportunities for a range of advice regarding courses, university systems, finance, accommodation, and general higher education expectations.

Supplementary tutoring

Supplementary tutoring for underprepared learners is a critical part of any student capacity development approach to support. All students, even those doing relatively well, can benefit from using supplementary tutors. An analysis of Indigenous students' use of tutors in our previous university, gathered from participant statements in the academic persistence study, revealed that students at different levels of capability use tutors for a range of different purposes and that their use of tutors tends to change over time as they work out how to learn and become more independent.[16]

A capacity development approach to Indigenous student support requires that staff actively allocate tutors as early as possible in the semester. Having a tutor from the very first week helps students avoid falling behind and gives them more time to develop their capacities, especially for conceptual understanding, academic skills, and more strategic ways of completing academic tasks. Waiting for students to ask for a tutor is to wait too long to provide the level of assistance many Indigenous students need to reduce their chances of failure or emotional distress. Many students have difficulty asking for assistance or leave it too late.[17]

It is also beneficial for the early allocation process if support staff know which students have a critical or likely need for a tutor before the teaching period begins. Establishing this requires knowledge of students' academic capacities or previous achievement outcomes and the subjects in which they are enrolled. For example, it is useful to consider categories of students most at risk of experiencing academic difficulties or failure as a basis for allocating tutors. This requires analysis of the subjects and courses in which Indigenous students experience frequent failures. Based on analyses and experiences, staff in our current university use the following categories for allocating tutors: all students enrolled in enabling programs, commencing students without all the prerequisite knowledge or skills assumed by the subjects in which they are enrolled, students enrolled in a math subject or a subject with a math component, students with low English proficiency and English as a second language to an Aboriginal or Torres Strait Islander language, students known to be at risk or not in good academic standing, students repeating a previously failed subject, and students enrolled in subjects known to have a high rate of Indigenous student failures in previous semesters.

When there has been a historically low uptake of tutors and/or a stigma attached to using them, we have found that just allocating students a tutor is not sufficient; support staff need to follow up to ensure students are using them and resolve any issues that prevent or discourage students from using them effectively. Although students cannot be forced to use a tutor, there is some justification for mandating the use of a tutor as a condition of entry for students identified as likely to need high levels of support. This further supports the argument for alternative entry diagnostic processes for selection-for-entry decisions and monitoring and tracking enrolled students.

In universities where there has been a stigma attached to using tutors, staff have found that including information about the benefits of supplementary tutoring in the orientation program helps normalise supplementary tutoring as a support 'you would be mad not to use,'[18] as one interviewee stated. When there is a need to recruit more tutors, orientation sessions for new tutors have also been reported as helpful for tutors to understand their roles. It also helps to provide clear information sheets for tutors and students about how to work together effectively and to request feedback regarding how the tutoring process is working so that changes can be made, if necessary. Further, staff need efficient administration systems and processes for managing the employment of tutors and monitoring whether the tutoring arrangement is effective. Monitoring is part of the academic support role to keep abreast of student progress and academic development. Online or electronic systems are beneficial for managing tutors and monitoring feedback.

In summary, any review of support services should closely examine the rates and patterns of supplementary tutor use by students and determine whether students who could benefit from tutors receive supplementary tutoring and whether tutoring is effective. Reviews should also determine what aspects of staff practices are in place and whether they are working or not working well. These aspects might include assessing those whose chances of success are most at risk if they do not have tutors, promoting the use of supplementary tutors for all students, allocating tutors in time for the commencement of the semester, preparing students and tutors for what is involved and what the benefits are, collecting tutor and student feedback to track how the tutoring process is functioning, and developing systems and processes for managing the administration of the scheme.

Managing Indigenous student diversity

There are over 20,000 Indigenous students in the university system nationally, with some universities having Indigenous student cohorts above a thousand. There is also increasing diversity within the Indigenous cohort in terms of individual students' socio-economic, cultural, and educational backgrounds, the widening range of disciplines, programs, and modes in which they study, and their career goals. Larger numbers and greater diversity within a university's Indigenous cohort provide extra challenges for staff to ensure all Indigenous students receive the level of support they require to succeed. Differences between universities' characteristics also mean the student support task can be more challenging in some universities than in others. These characteristics include differences in universities' locations and primary student catchment areas, selection methods and cut-offs for Indigenous student entry, and resources and abilities to attract higher-achieving Indigenous students with scholarships and on-campus accommodation. The dispersal of Indigenous students across multi-campus sites of some universities adds to the challenges of supporting Indigenous students in those universities. Universities with significant numbers of Indigenous students undertaking external, away-from-home, or remote area studies also face additional challenges in providing support to these students. Universities with Indigenous students for whom English is a second language to an Aboriginal or Torres Strait Islander language have further challenges, which are often compounded by Indigenous–Western knowledge (and logic) relations in the academic sphere.

The diversity within cohorts has implications for student support tasks, how they are organised across universities or within IEUs, how students' needs for support are identified, what sort of information staff need to support increasing numbers, and how staff might maintain a sense of Indigenous community and belonging. The diverse situations of different universities highlight the need for locally devised strategies to manage the specifics of more complex situations, particularly for universities where members of cohorts are studying in a range of modes, that are required to service regional and remote communities, and that have larger numbers of Indigenous students in enabling pathways from workplaces, TAFE, and non-Australian Tertiary Admission Rank tracks. The increased diversity within the Indigenous student cohorts suggests that those who provide and deliver support cannot predict or assess the support needs of *all* Indigenous students based on general assumptions about Indigenous students as a singular category distinct from other students.

Support staff must understand more about the differences between their individual Indigenous students and how they might affect a student's chances of success. That presupposes knowledge about *all* the students in a university's Indigenous cohort. The diverse characteristics within the national cohort also have implications for differences between cohorts in different universities. In some cases and university contexts, students' cultural and language backgrounds related to remoteness and English language proficiency will be extremely relevant to providing support but may be less relevant in others. There may be significant cohorts of Indigenous students in disciplines with high student contact hours or degrees of difficulty, such as medicine, law, and engineering, that warrant a specialised approach for supporting those students in close cooperation with the faculties (and some residential colleges) in those universities. External Indigenous students are often overlooked, even though they have always had a presence in many universities. These cohorts have specific challenges and support needs associated with being off campus. Differences such as these suggest that support strategies, processes, and systems for managing students will require a significant degree of customisation to suit each specific university and cohort, as the Review stated.[19]

The increasing diversity within Indigenous cohorts also raises management issues concerning the discourse on Indigenous student identity and staff attitudes and assumptions about students' expressions of their Indigenous identity. In our experience, staff attitudes and assumptions, which are often based on superficial knowledge or observations of student behaviours, can influence how the support staff interact with Indigenous students from different backgrounds, and the degree or quality of support they offer.

Indigenous students (and staff) express their Aboriginal and Torres Strait Islander identities in different ways depending on the historical journeys of their families and communities during and since the colonisation of Australia, and their own life experiences and circumstances. While undertaking their degrees, some students will be more pressed to prioritise developing their student identities in preparation for assuming professional identities. For others, their Indigenous identities will take priority in all their interactions in classrooms and the wider university environment. Further, some students will be politically active and involved in community affairs and causes, while others will defer that contribution until after completing their studies or gaining experience in their respective professions. Most students are actively determining how to reconcile their Indigenous obligations and identities with their professional aspirations, obligations, and identities in the future.

The assumptions and attitudes of staff about students are reflected in the way staff respond to some students and not others and these responses can and do influence whether students continue to visit the IEU or ask for help. Not all staff have sufficient understanding of the diversity of Indigenous Australians' historical experiences or their background stories and journeys to reflect on the issues of diversity in their support practices. We have had numerous experiences of staff rushing to judgements based on a lack of knowledge about particular students or categories of students. The time has passed when support staff could assume that any Indigenous student they do not personally know is tainted by suspicions of inauthenticity.

Given the growing diversity within Indigenous cohorts, any thinking about services should consider how well the organisation and delivery of support strategies can respond to all students' needs and whether staff practices are inclusive of all students, whatever their cultural backgrounds, future goals, identity expressions, and modes of study. The increased diversity of Indigenous cohorts can be wielded in arguments for change to emphasise the importance of not making assumptions or judgements about students that lead to the neglect of some students' needs. It also supports an argument for supporting all students, not just those who ask for help.

Managing student progress

Monitoring and tracking systems and processes were discussed in more detail in Chapter 2. Monitoring and tracking individual students is a central component of a student success and capacity development approach. Managers wanting to develop systems and processes for monitoring and tracking individual student progress should consider what is required to develop and implement a system. This will include considering what sort of student information needs to be known and accessed or recorded by staff, what sort of staff activities will contribute to effective monitoring and tracking and how individual tracking and increased support responses will affect staff workloads, staff–student ratios, staff qualifications, and staff roles and responsibilities. Also necessary to consider is the information required to assess the effectiveness of monitoring and tracking systems and processes and the areas for improving support practices, what sort of training and professional development staff might need to implement individual tracking and monitoring processes, and how to instigate a 'plan, do, report, reflect, review and change cycle' to enable continual improvements or adjustments to strategies and practices.

Developing semester schedules for support tasks and interventions

Effective and efficient student support does not only occur during the teaching period or individually with students through a monitoring and tracking process. A capacity development approach must involve determining the key dates in the annual student calendar and what these might indicate for the students' learning journeys and support needs before, during, and after the teaching and exam periods. This is particularly important when considering the journey of commencing students and the capabilities that higher education learning requires (see Chapter 1). While a monitoring and tracking process provides a method for supporting individual students through a semester, staff must also consider the sequence and timing of other activities and interventions for groups of students who have similar needs at similar times. For prospective students, this might be managed using a schedule for staff activities associated with planning and delivering outreach, pre-entry, and selection-for-entry activities. For commencing and continuing students, staff activities are more likely to involve information dissemination and practical assistance at different times before commencement, during the semester, and after the teaching and exam periods. Key dates in university and student calendars provide a starting point from which student support managers and their staff can develop staff semester and annual activity calendars and schedules, including the lead-in times needed for decision-making, development and planning of staff activities, and interventions.

However, other factors are also involved in planning considerations. For example, for commencing students, this might involve determining how students' needs for preparation and assistance relate to the key dates in their academic calendars, what sorts of knowledge and practical planning, academic skills, and strategies students need to be aware of and when they need to be aware of them, and what sort of support they may require to develop these at particular points before, during, and after the teaching and exam periods. This requires information about students, their courses and key dates, and their prior educational attainments. It also requires a sound understanding of the self-regulated learning processes and various influences on students' chances of success (see Chapter 1). In this process, it is helpful to think about what sort of common needs arise for all students and students in particular disciplines, courses, or subjects and what sort of needs can only be met promptly through individual support. This process should enable staff to begin considering whether to develop group interventions, when to provide them, and when to follow up on students' needs individually.

These considerations make it easier to sequence activities and develop schedules for activities such as group outreach, pre-entry programs, and selection-for-entry programs for prospective students; individual course guidance and assistance during the enrolment process, group orientation programs or workshops before the commencement of the teaching period or during the exam study period; regular contact schedules for ongoing individual support during the teaching and exam periods for enrolled students; and follow-up activities to support individual students after their exam results, either to counsel and guide the students' next steps or to develop their abilities to interpret and learn from feedback. Together, these steps provide a basis for some thoughtful planning of staff-initiated activities to support students proactively and efficiently.

Planning and scheduling activities also involve staff being aware of the emotional and social aspects of the higher education journey for students at different points before, during, and after the teaching and exam periods. For commencing students, in particular, entering a new and unfamiliar environment and engaging with new and unfamiliar knowledge and methods of teaching and learning is daunting, especially when they are also academically underprepared. For many Indigenous students, this experience is often made more challenging by relocating and being away from home for the first time, without familiar social supports, and coping with uncertain financial circumstances. In these situations, students are easily overwhelmed by feelings of uncertainty about their futures and whether they can handle the demands. Some of these students will decide to leave early or begin thinking about leaving at critical points in the semester; thus, they require timely support.

Conversely, underprepared students, especially commencing students, can be easily overwhelmed and panicked if they are overloaded with information and advice all at once. Therefore, support staff must consider how to stage their dissemination of information and any support tasks, activities, or interventions so that they are digestible and well-timed to coincide with students' most urgent needs. This staging is especially important between students' acceptance of offers and the first few weeks of the teaching period.

The structure of an activities schedule will depend on the specific context and Indigenous student cohorts within each university. Various issues and factors have to be worked through in context; thus, there is no substitute for careful thinking and sound knowledge about students' needs.

Developing help-seeking behaviours

The discussions of the key concepts in Chapter 1 emphasised the importance of students' help-seeking behaviours when strengthening their self-efficacy beliefs, developing the competencies of self-regulated learners, and experiencing challenges and setbacks associated with learning or personal circumstances and issues. Ensuring students receive adequate support when they need it requires some thoughtful consideration about how to encourage students' active help-seeking behaviours and what changes that might imply for the way support is delivered. Before doing so, we found it helpful to examine some established attitudes and practices currently in use so that staff could understand the limits of some practices.

The actual work of supporting individual students in need of assistance has traditionally relied on individual students asking for help when needed. Not all students who need help ask for help or find it easy to ask for help. Overwhelmed, commencing students can have difficulty identifying where to begin, what they need help with, whom to go to for help, or how to ask for help. Some students do not ask for help because they feel stupid or ashamed, think they should be able to work things out for themselves, or worry about wasting staff time when they perceive that other students need more help than they do.[20] Many students wait so long before asking for help that subject failures or withdrawal from their studies cannot be avoided. Providing support only for those who actively seek it means many Indigenous students who require assistance will not receive it and that many more will not receive support in time to avoid extreme emotional distress, subject failures, or withdrawal from their studies.

In our experience, arguments are sometimes made by support staff and managers that Indigenous students are responsible for their own learning and that asking for help is part of taking responsibility. This argument is dismissive and shows a limited understanding of the effects of under-preparation for higher education on many commencing Indigenous students and the many reasons why Indigenous students feel unable to ask for help. The argument also shows a limited understanding of how difficult it can be for higher-achieving commencing and later-year Indigenous students to admit they need help.

Conversely, anecdotal reporting over the years suggests that some students display an overdeveloped sense of entitlement to assistance, expressed in expectations that support staff or supplementary tutors will do tasks for them. It is a disservice to students to do things for them rather than assist them to work out how to do things for themselves. Assisting students will often involve staff demonstrating or modelling how to do things and some 'hand-holding' to build their confidence; however, there is a discernible line between that sort of assistance and yielding to student requests to do tasks for them. The latter promotes dependence rather than the benefits of learning and achieving from one's own efforts, supported by guidance and encouragement from others.

One way to overcome student reluctance to ask for assistance is to normalise help-seeking behaviours for all students. Normalising support as something available for all students and not just those at risk of failure makes it easier for all students to seek help for matters big and small. Normalising support as something that all students can benefit from requires that staff convey the message to all students. Building relationships with individual students or course/disciplinary cohorts helps students feel at ease and safe when asking for help. This, in turn, implies direct staff contact with *all* students to establish secure and trusting relationships. Without building relationships with students, many students may still not come forward for assistance. However, emails and mentions in non-compulsory orientation programs are not enough to build the confidence of some students to come forward. In our previous university, a 'use all the support you can' message was emphasised in the Indigenous orientation program, the early learning interviews the academic support staff conducted with all commencing students, and through a student contact strategy during the first few weeks of each semester by academic and pastoral support staff. In our current university, a similar contact strategy is a major component of the ongoing monitoring and tracking process and individual student case management approach.

Student responsibility can be developed over time if students are well informed and confident in their relationships with support staff. Student responsibility can also be developed if students' engagements with support staff lead them to understand the value and benefits of seeking support. Support practices should enable students to learn that they can improve their learning outcomes by combining their own efforts with the available assistance.

Rethinking academic and pastoral support roles

A capacity development approach to Indigenous student support highlights the need for individualised support. This is based on understanding the implications of the key concepts associated with student success and study conditions discussed in Chapter 1. These discussions highlight how academic success in higher education involves a complex interplay between individual student, institutional and external factors, and students' abilities to integrate cognitive, metacognitive, motivational, and affective skills for successful independent learning. Individualised support implies the need for better monitoring of student progress. Further, monitoring and tracking students have implications for how pastoral and academic support roles relate to each other. Whichever way Indigenous pastoral (personal, social, and cultural) support and academic support are organised (e.g., from within faculties, university services, or IEUs), reconsidering how staff work together to resolve a student's issues and provide effective support is useful in any review of the effectiveness of support practices.

Individualised support involves much more than just contacting and helping individual students. Support staff responses must recognise and respond to the interplay of academic and non-academic factors that affect individual Indigenous students and their ability to achieve success or stay in their studies. Academic and pastoral support interventions often need to occur simultaneously to keep students in their studies and decrease their risk of failing. For example, students often present with an academic challenge that is the outcome of challenging personal circumstances. On the other hand, students often present with adverse personal circumstances or setbacks that are likely to affect their academic progress. In other cases, students may present with issues related to academic learning or lecturer/tutorial/peer interactions that can affect their learning, emotional wellbeing, and/ or personal lives. All these situations can lead to disengagement from learning, subject failures, or decisions to leave. Whatever the case, there is a strong argument for early and close communication between pastoral and academic support staff to ensure the student is wholly supported, both personally and academically, in a way that will enable them to continue their studies with the least possible effects on their academic progress. This highlights the need for more integrated forms of academic and pastoral support.

In our previous university, apart from the recruitment and supplementary tutor administration officers, the support team consisted of several pastoral support staff and one part-time, in-house academic tutor, with most of the academic support provided by supplementary tutors. The change process included appointing a matching number of academic support advisers. Suitably qualified academic support staff are more equipped to effectively engage in academic discourse with students (and faculty academics) and plan academic support interventions. These two teams worked separately but shared information through face-to-face contact (made easier in an open-area office) and the use of Microsoft Excel spreadsheets to record updated information and support responses.

In our current university, some role restructuring and appointment of academic support advisers alongside pastoral support staff were required. During the change process, academic and pastoral support staff were organised into teams of two, consisting of one academic support adviser and one pastoral support adviser. The subsequent development of an open-area workspace now enables academic and pastoral members of each team to work alongside each other. All teams address a roughly equal share of the full Indigenous student cohort based on disciplinary and course lines or combinations where necessary. Both members of these pairs share information and some aspects of their roles but remain primarily responsible for undertaking distinct duties associated with their primary academic and pastoral roles. This is the best arrangement we have implemented so far. Currently, a team of two is responsible for approximately 130 students.

In both these arrangements in the two different universities, the teams were/are responsible for monitoring and tracking students so that they receive timely support that develops their capacities to gradually take charge of their own learning and become more independent. In both situations, non-Indigenous academic support advisers have been employed alongside Indigenous pastoral support staff (most in our previous university and a minority in the present one). This situation reflected the difficulty of finding suitably qualified Indigenous academic support staff at the time. The presence of non-Indigenous academic advisers initially caused anxiety for Indigenous staff in both situations. Managers in these situations must be clear about the temporary inclusion of non-Indigenous staff with expertise in disciplines (e.g., psychology graduates schooled in statistics) where IEUs cannot recruit an Indigenous person with the right skill set.

The main benefit of working in pairs with a fixed student cohort is that it increases the sharing of information about individual students so that both staff members receive a more comprehensive understanding of students' changing circumstances, progress, and support needs. This fuller understanding of students by both members of the teams enables each to tailor their interventions to be more mindful of intersecting issues. Sharing information about academic and pastoral needs enables the team to develop integrated ILSPs (see Chapter 2). These plans consolidate the individual student issues each team member needs to focus on throughout the semester and allow each staff member to know what the other is doing regarding a student. Importantly, when teams remain in charge of the same student cohorts, this consistency helps build familiarity and reliable relationships between students and staff throughout their studies. It also enables staff to build more specialised knowledge about the specific disciplines, courses, and subjects that their students study than they would if students were allotted randomly or in year levels. This arrangement also enables teams to develop relationships within the relevant faculty.

Two-member teams also enable one of the team members to be available for students through recreation leave and other absences while also allowing for referrals to other academic/pastoral advisers if necessary. Simultaneously, a paired arrangement still enables each team member to liaise with other academic or pastoral support staff concerning student issues and staff challenges in those distinct areas.

However, there are possible risks when staff work in pairs with a fixed student cohort. The distinctive aspects of the two roles may become blurred unless these have been clearly defined. A team may also be tempted to depart from the overall support goals and whole-of-support approach, strategies, systems, and processes in favour of doing things their own way. Further, there is always the possibility of personality and style clashes arising between the two team members, leading to decreased sharing of information and planning, and the increased possibility of contradictory advice that may confuse students.

These benefits and risks identify areas that will require management. Appropriate organisation of office spaces for team operations is another area requiring planning and management. Staff will also benefit from clarity about their distinct roles and areas of overlap. In our current university, the shared and distinct aspects of academic and pastoral support roles and responsibilities have been provided in information sheets for staff.

Managing tensions between Indigenous cultural values and institutional/professional cultures and practices

In addition to assisting Indigenous students, IEUs strive to generate a sense of community for their students within the wider university community. Support centres and relationships with staff offer students a place of safety and refuge. This is a key element to many (but not all) Indigenous students' sense of belonging and the development of their confidence for interactions in other sections of the university. Cultural support for Indigenous students takes different forms and levels of emphasis in different IEUs across the country; however, it generally includes activities that mark significant events or days on the Indigenous calendar, social and cultural activities for Indigenous students, and the appointment of Elders in residence as cultural reference points for Indigenous students and staff. The provision of cultural support also includes using culturally familiar ways of relating to, communicating, and interacting with Indigenous students.

A capacity development approach to student support does not necessarily imply changes for an IEU's cultural support activities. The exceptions are when students' participation in additional activities unduly reduces the time that some individual students require for their studies to succeed or when staff organisation of additional activities for students takes too much time away from more pressing aspects of the support process.

However, a capacity development approach does highlight some tensions. In particular, this approach has implications for how staff integrate Indigenous cultural practices into their student support practices and work cultures. In some workplaces, the increased workload that comes with monitoring *all* Indigenous students will require adjustments to workplace practices that are understood to be cultural practices. Thus, in any change process, it is important to consider what sorts of cultural–professional tensions are likely to arise when implementing a student capacity development approach.

One example of such tension is the practice of 'yarning' as a form of social support for Indigenous students. Yarning is an Indigenous concept and style of communication that expresses and reinforces connectedness, relatedness, and trust in supportive staff–student relationships; these are essential cultural values for support practices. As a support practice, yarning may not necessarily address an immediate academic or personal support need; however, this familiar way of relating benefits the students' sense of security in their relationships with staff and forms an important element of emotional and social support. Having secure relationships with those who provide accurate feedback can be important for some students' motivation to persist through challenges.[21] Therefore, as a cultural communication style, yarning practices provide more than just information transmission between students and staff. Thus, maintaining this cultural practice is not just about Indigenous people's cultural continuity, but also its benefits for students, particularly those who feel isolated, 'out of place,' or have not yet developed social support networks at university.

Although many staff handle the tensions between cultural and professional practice very well, there are some extreme (but not so uncommon) situations where tensions or conflicts are likely to arise between Indigenous cultural practices and professional workplace cultures. One is when yarning practice legitimates students taking up residence in staff offices for long periods, with the practice being justified as a cultural practice or 'our way.' Another is when the close relationships between students and staff lead to staff involving students in workplace issues or university business and politics, either inadvertently or to solicit students to agitate or protest. The first example takes staff time away from other students and aspects of the staff member's role; the second takes time away from students—time they need for learning and study purposes. Further, students being in staff offices for lengthy periods increases the risk of being exposed to confidential information about other students or hearing phone conversations they should not hear, which has implications for professional ethics associated with student privacy and confidentiality.

A capacity development approach requires staff to keep abreast of the needs of *all* students in the cohort for which they are responsible. If staff do not organise their time or are not mindful of the needs of all their students, they will not fulfil their professional obligations to all students. One way to ease these tensions is to understand Indigenous cultural values and practices and institutional, professional values and practices in terms of their synergies rather than their differences or uniqueness. Including cultural values and practices adds an important, if not critical, element to professional ethics and practices; professional practices add an important element to staff cultural practices. In the context of an individualised capacity development approach, professional ethics help direct work cultures dedicated to *all* students, not just those whose sense of place and cultural comfort is the IEU. The cultural aspect prevents professional practices from becoming too formal or detached. The professional aspect discourages favouring some students and neglecting others in need of assistance. The cultural aspect provides the familiar and comforting form of Aboriginal and Torres Strait Islander relatedness. Using cultural and professional support practices together provides a model for students' own navigation of Indigenous and professional values in their future professions.

How these synergies will work in practice will be specific to the university and dependent on the characteristics of the Indigenous cohort. In our previous and current universities, these issues have been partly addressed by placing staff in open offices behind glass so that students have to ask at the reception to see a staff member and the staff member had to meet students in the student study area or a private withdrawal room. Being behind glass and meeting students in the study area increased the visibility of staff who had previously been housed in separate air-conditioned offices behind solid doors. In the changed arrangement, staff cannot reach their offices without walking through the student area, which helps to increase incidental student–staff contact. While there was initial anxiety about this shift, in practice, these anxieties were soon allayed.

Establishing an ethic of care for all Indigenous students

There is still the question of how to integrate Indigenous cultural values into the professional delivery of student support services. A family model as an ethic of care was implicitly practised in our previous university, led by the then student support manager and staff. Versions of a family model are likely implicitly practised in many IEUs around the country. In the capacity development approach, we have made this family cultural model an *explicit* model for professional practice, being mindful of the goals of student success and the development of independent learners.

A family model of care considers the entire Indigenous cohort of students and the student support staff as one extended family. Staff think of the students as they would their own and support them out of a sense of family 'love and care' for them and their futures. In the event of disagreements among staff about procedures or practices, the basis of resolution is 'what is in the best interests of students and their futures.' Students are asked to treat each other, staff, and tutors with respect, look out for their Indigenous student peers, and help inexperienced students by passing on the benefits of the assistance they have received.

This model engenders a positive atmosphere in the support centre, positive staff dispositions towards all students, and positive student dispositions towards staff and other students. The cultural aspect prevents the professional practice from becoming too formal or detached. The professional aspect discourages favouring some students and neglecting others in need of assistance.

Evaluate, reflect, review, plan, and improve cycles

Any approach to improving the effectiveness of Indigenous student support services and practices needs to evaluate the outcomes of any changes to support staff services and practices. Student outcomes data, alongside data about specific support strategies and support staff actions, can be used by staff to reflect on and evaluate whether their efforts are helping students' outcomes and study experiences. This local data analysis aims to identify where further reviews and developments of strategies, systems, and processes are indicated to improve student outcomes. Analysis of individual student outcome data each semester also provides essential information to help staff develop ILSPs for the upcoming semester.

All universities and most IEUs will have a practice of annually reporting students' outcomes to the Australian Government; however, many may be less practised in utilising this information to review and adjust their support strategies and systems. In our experience, many reflective support staff members are aware of the limitations of their practices but are not sure how to improve them, particularly if there is little support for their ideas from other staff and managers. In some IEUs, there are likely to be members of staff who do not have a practice of reflecting on their own practices or the effectiveness of what they do for students.

A strong, non-threatening case for local data analysis and semester reporting must be proposed to staff. Because it has implications for staff workloads and their sense of competency, the case needs to emphasise the aim of improving student outcomes and not that of evaluating individual staff performance. The individual staff performance process needs to be kept very separate from the data analysis process. Reporting sessions should be non-judgemental and pivoted towards constructive and cooperative problem-solving. In reporting and planning sessions, support staff need opportunities to discuss student and support issues, and they need to have some ownership over the solutions for improving strategies and practices. However, care should be taken that these sessions do not degenerate into lengthy discussions about everything that is wrong in the university or with students; the focus must be on what the analysis of student outcomes and staff actions might indicate for future changes to staff practices. These sessions need to be planned and timed, staff need sufficient time to prepare their reports beforehand, and sessions need to be led by a strong but sensitive facilitator. Student support managers should also report their activities and overall student progress and support centre activity in these sessions.

In our experience and collaborations with other universities, managers and staff who are serious about doing the best for students appreciate what data analytics reveal about students and their strategies and practices. They quickly learn to build reports and share their reflections on their practices without any defensiveness. They appreciate the stimulation that comes from having some focused time to share problems and ideas with others and develop adjusted or additional strategies. Support staff in our current university meet beforehand to discuss the format of semester reports so that there is consistent reporting across all the teams. Their presentations are no more than 5 or 10 minutes long, followed by a period for engagement with the group regarding effectiveness and areas for improvement.

Information about the outcomes of the individual team's student cohort is included in these reports. Some of this information includes general summaries and comments on academic and personal issues that impeded student success and staff strategies and interventions that were helpful or did not work so well. Other information statistically details things such as student withdrawals, completions, grades, and success rates, including the numbers of failures, passes, credits, distinctions, and high distinctions; student standing and status, including outstanding student results, such as supplementary exams and extensions; the relative outcomes of different degree cohorts; the subjects with the highest failure rates; the number of students who used supplementary tutors; and the number of hours of tutoring students used. These are generally compiled for each disciplinary cohort that the support team is responsible for.

Presentations also include staff reflections on what strategies they think worked well and any indicated areas to adjust or try different strategies. Comparing a semester's result with that of the previous semester or frequently failed subjects in the previous year assists teams' evaluations and reflections. These reports have been growing more sophisticated during the four years staff have been reporting in our current university, aided by the student case management software that has been developed for this purpose. The analytical reflections of staff have also grown more sophisticated, with staff thoughtfully identifying the issues requiring attention, the strategies and practices needing adjustments or developments, and their ideas about what effect these changes will have.

Building support staff knowledge about Indigenous students and their circumstances

It has been our experience of support practices in three universities, and in others that the primary author has reviewed, that support staff and managers have not always known how many Indigenous students attend their university, the numbers in different disciplines or courses, or how many are in preparation, undergraduate, and postgraduate programs. Further, staff have not always known what year level their undergraduate students are or their rate of subject success or progress towards completion. Staff have not always known how many years some students have been studying and how many times they have changed courses or their reasons for doing so. Staff have not always known how many times a student has attempted, failed, or repeated a subject. Staff may also be unaware of students who are thinking about leaving or students who have withdrawn from their studies and the reasons for these thoughts and actions. In some cases, staff have not known how to access such information, at least not in a useful format.

In these circumstances, staff have little way of knowing how all students are going and who requires support. This situation does seem to be changing, at least in some universities, as the monitoring, tracking, and case management discourses take hold.[22] Nevertheless, in some universities, keeping abreast of changes in student circumstances still often relies largely on Indigenous students to initiate contact with staff. Further, in our experience, many staff only know the students who voluntarily present themselves to the support centre, IEU, or services provided by faculties or university student services.

Support staff require access to relevant and current sources of student information to ensure students who need support receive the support they need during their studies. Not knowing all students, their disciplines, and courses or how they are progressing can lead to a failure to identify and support *all* students who require academic assistance. Not knowing all students, their financial, accommodation, health and wellbeing, and personal challenges can lead to a failure to identify and support *all* students who require pastoral, personal, or cultural support to continue their studies. Not keeping abreast of changes in student progress and circumstances risks students slipping through the support net. Developing systems and processes for staff to access current student information is an essential component of effective student support. The absence of these indicates a need to rethink the way support is managed.

Professional ethics and student privacy and confidentiality

A capacity development approach that monitors and tracks individual students will necessitate access to and collection of a significant amount of student data and information and records related to the nature of students' challenges and staff responses. Therefore, maintaining student privacy and confidentiality is a serious issue that indicates the need for professional development. This professional development should include knowledge of and compliance with the relevant university policies.

However, staff knowledge and compliance must also be reflected in the day-to-day way staff discuss and share information about students' challenges and their own interactions with them. An important part of a manager's role is to establish boundaries concerning, for example, student information that is confidential, sensitive, or personal. A simple rule is for staff to only share information with each other, other teams, or others in the university on a 'needs to know' basis. However, the guide to avoiding unprofessional practice is that no student information should be shared among staff through casual or gossipy conversations. In Indigenous student support, the lines between casual and support-related conversations, staff and students, and between staff members themselves are sometimes blurry. This is because many students are often already known to staff outside the university, belong to families known to staff or are related to staff. Nevertheless, staff need to be reminded to be cautious about what information they share with other staff members, people outside the immediate workplace, or other students.

It is important to maintain a record of significant and sensitive student incidents or issues in case this information may be useful for advocating for or defending a student in the future. However, entries such as 'confidential personal issue' or 'distressing interaction in a class or with a person' are sufficient to indicate a previous significant event, along with the action that was taken, for example, 'talked to the student, suggested referral to the counsellor; phoned and emailed x at x to set up a meeting to discuss student issue on x date,' with a further follow-up of the outcome. The systems and processes that staff use to record student information also need assessments to determine how widely different sorts of student information can be shared and to institute mechanisms to restrict who can access confidential and other student information. The case management platform that staff use in our current university can restrict access to student information in this way.

Professional development

The changes and adjustments for shifting practices towards a capacity development approach require professional development in seven areas. Decision-making in this area will depend on the specific context of support arrangements and student cohorts in each university:

1   background knowledge associated with the key concepts relevant to student success and independent learning, particularly concerning the effects of academic under-preparation and capabilities of independent learners
2   procedural and process knowledge associated with university admissions, pathways, course progression rules, and student management systems
3   monitoring, tracking, individual student case management, and how to develop and use the various systems, strategies, and processes that underpin effective monitoring and tracking
4   analysing student data for reporting, reviews, strategy adjustments, and planning
5   building staff awareness regarding how they integrate cultural and professional work cultures and practices
6   ethics and protocols for student privacy and confidentiality, the management of student data, and university compliance issues
7   appropriate language use by staff when prompting students to discuss their personal and academic challenges (included because some staff we know have raised this issue regarding assisting students with emotional issues—staff must be aware of the boundaries and sensitivities of language and communication involved when trying to establish how to assist a student).

Professional development requires forethought. Any topics for professional development are best presented at appropriate times during the change process so that staff can learn and apply them directly and present their feedback to the managers. We suggest professional development is best conducted in stages as needs arise concerning certain changes; too much information at once can overwhelm the staff. Some professional development can be delivered during the general course of staff meetings; others may require expertise from elsewhere or be the subject of workshops. Semester review and planning days provide opportunities for professional development or, at the very least, identifying staff needs for professional development.

Developing an argument for change

One or more of all the key aspects of supporting students along the educational journey, which have been discussed in this chapter, may indicate areas for change or adjustments to strategies and practices. Areas of possible change can be identified through a *review and audit process of the current support strategies and student outcomes* in the local student and support context to determine where improvements are indicated. The review findings should give student support managers and others committed to improving Indigenous student support practices sufficient information to develop an argument for change and the proposals and priorities for changes. We suggest that a manager should have a strong understanding of all the information gathered in the analysis of the local situation to present a case for changes designed to improve the effectiveness of student support organisations, strategies, and delivery practices. This is the case irrespective of whether the review is conducted by a manager or an external person.

The local situation analysis should optimally occur against the background knowledge of what is involved in the higher education learning process and students' study conditions, health, and wellbeing.[23] A manager can also use other imperatives to strengthen their arguments, for example, Indigenous students' levels of readiness/under-preparation for higher education success, policy imperatives related to student outcomes targets, and the growing financial debts of Indigenous students due to repeated subject failures, which impose future burdens on Indigenous individuals, families, and communities in general. Other imperatives may emerge in specific universities, disciplines, and Indigenous student cohorts.

The case for change needs to be developed before considering how to implement any changes. In our experience, staff need to fully understand why they are being asked to change their practices.

Managing the change process

Creating change at the practice level is not an easy or quick process and is not easy to sustain in the event of leadership changes; this is something we have learnt the hard way through reform efforts in three universities over the last two decades. Where student support practices are well entrenched, it can take time for changes to be established and consolidated. At the very least, particularly during the initial stages, changes cause many anxieties for staff and doubts and uncertainties about the 'why,' 'what,' and 'how' and the possible outcomes of doing things differently. In some cases, questioning established practices can provoke defensiveness and risk resistance from staff. If mismanaged, the change process can provoke resentment and half-levels of commitment from staff, at best.

A planned process for managing change is more likely to reduce staff anxieties if the reasons for change are explained and the goals of student support firmly established and explained. The change process works best if it encourages staff input and involvement and works with their considerable knowledge and experience of students in their specific university context. Simultaneously, the change process must improve staff knowledge and help them rethink their approaches to student support; thus, staff input and managerial direction must be carefully balanced.

For support staff, the process of changing practices to support the goals of success and capacity development involves professional development and the development of their capacities to manage new systems and processes. Therefore, change processes take time and do not happen overnight or by managerial imposition followed by a quick leadership exit.

We have found that sustaining changes over time while continuing to develop staff practices requires focused and consistent leadership; helpful but not overwhelming professional development delivered in a staged process; space (and support) for staff to trial, adjust, and practice new skills, processes, and operational systems in a way that is manageable, not overwhelming, and that builds confidence; constructive feedback to staff during this process; avoiding negative judgements of staff efforts when progress has been difficult to achieve; and respecting staff feedback. Support staff also need to be convinced of the value of their actions, which is best achieved by tracking improvements in local student outcomes. This requires relevant data collection and analytics to gauge the effectiveness of staff strategies and efforts and to provide useful feedback for further adjustment of practices. Small and incremental improvements encourage staff beliefs in their competencies, sustain their motivation to make incremental improvements, encourage them to evaluate their progress through reflections on their functioning, as well as external feedback, and help them sustain their persistence and resilience in the face of inevitable challenges and setbacks, as well as their commitment to pursuing set goals. That is, for staff, the change process involves learning to develop and apply new knowledge, skills, and strategies and, as for students, the approach needs to be strengths-based.

How professional development is staged over time depends on the specific context and degree of changes required. We have learnt through experience that staff need time to process the rationales for and practical details of changes. In our experience, support staff are more positive regarding change when they feel confident about their actions and can witness the benefits of these actions for students. Inductions for new staff are essential for keeping a capacity development and individual case management approach on track. Like teaching, providing effective support is part science and part art and intuition. While individual staff will always bring their own style to their support practices, it is important that all staff work towards the same goals and approaches and that their practices are informed by the necessary knowledge sets and conform to the systems and processes established to deliver efficiencies.

Our main caution about the change process is to expect that implementing major changes to the support approach, staff practices, and systems and processes for efficient delivery of services may take several years. In our current university, this process has been progressing for almost five years, involving a restructuring of staff roles, the gradual recruitment of staff with educational or academic backgrounds, professional development, and learning to operate with new systems and processes. While selection-for-entry processes and pre-entry programs for school students have been established, there is still much work to be done in outreach to schools in the lower-secondary and upper-primary years, as well as the alignment of enabling and transition pathways leading into undergraduate studies. Budgetary considerations will likely lengthen the time needed in some universities. Strong, sustained, and informed leadership is essential to the process. Oversight across staff involved in the support process is also essential; however, it must be minimal or structured through meetings and, we cannot emphasise enough, constructive and productive at all times.

Notes

1 See, e.g., Walker, 2000.
2 This goal is consistent with the Review's definition of student success; see Behrendt et al., 2012.
3 Burke et al., 2016, p. 7.
4 Department of Employment, Education and Training, 1989.
5 See Chapter 1 sections: 'Self-efficacy and academic self-efficacy'; 'Self-regulation'; 'Persistence'; 'Motivation and persistence.'
6 Stebleton et al., 2012.
7 Lopez & Louis, 2009.
8 Lopez & Louis, 2009.
9 Gray, 2018.
10 See the section 'Finding a frame for the student support approach' in this chapter.
11 See the section 'Defining goals for Indigenous student support practices' in this chapter.
12 See the section 'Finding a frame for the student support approach' in this chapter.
13 For a typology of interventions across this journey, see Naylor et al., 2013.
14 The Review noted that more than half of Indigenous students entered higher education in this way; see Behrendt et al., 2012, p. 49.
15 Fredericks et al., 2015.
16 See Nakata et al., 2019.
17 See the section 'Developing students' help-seeking behaviours' in this chapter; see also the section 'Self-regulation' in Chapter 1 for the importance of help-seeking behaviours for becoming an independent learner.
18 See Nakata et al., 2019.
19 Behrendt et al., 2012, p. 57.
20 See, e.g., Barney, 2016; Pechenkina, 2015, Penfold, 1996

21 For self-determination motivation theory, see Ryan & Deci, 2000, s. 1.
22 See, e.g., Universities Australia, 2019, pp. 22–31.
23 See Chapter 1.

References

Barney, K. (2016). Listening to and learning from the experiences of Aboriginal and Torres Strait Islander students to facilitate success. *Student Success*, 7(1), 1–11. https://doi.org/10.5204/ssj.v7i1.317

Behrendt, L., Larkin, S., Griew, R. & Kelly, P. (2012, July). *Review of higher education, access and outcomes for Aboriginal and Torres Strait Islander People final report*. Australian Government. https://www.dese.gov.au/aboriginal-and-torres-strait-islander-higher-education/review-higher-education-access-and-outcomes-aboriginal-and-torres-strait-islander-people

Burke, P. J., Bennett, A., Burgess, C., Gray, K. & Southgate, E. (2016). *Capability, belonging and equity in higher education: Developing inclusive approaches*. University of Newcastle. https://nova.newcastle.edu.au/vital/access/manager/Repository/uon:32939

Department of Employment, Education and Training. (1989). *National Aboriginal and Torres Strait Islander education policy: Joint policy statement*. Australian Government Publishing Service. http://hdl.voced.edu.au/10707/81579

Fredericks, B., Kinnear, S., Daniels, C., CroftWarcon, P. & Mann, J. (2015). *Path+ways: Towards best practice in Indigenous access education*. National Centre for Student Equity in Higher Education. https://www.ncsehe.edu.au/publications/pathways-towards-best-practice-bridging-indigenous-participation-regional-dual-sector-universities/

Gray, M. (2018). Back to basics: A critique of the strengths perspective in social work. *Families in Society: The Journal of Contemporary Social Services*, *92*(1), 5–11. https://doi.org/10.1606/1044-3894.4054

Lopez, S. J. & Louis, M. C. (2009). The principles of strengths-based education. *Journal of College and Character*, *10*(4). https://doi.org/10.2202/1940-1639.1041

Nakata, M., Nakata, V., Day, A., Martin, G. & Peachey, M. (2019). Indigenous undergraduates' use of supplementary tutors: Developing academic capabilities for success in higher education studies. *Australian Journal of Indigenous Education*, *48*(2), 119–128. https://doi.org/10.1017/jie.2017.39

Naylor, R., Baik, C. & James, R. (2013, August). *A critical intervention framework for advancing equity in Australian higher education: Report prepared for the Department of Industry, Innovation, Climate Change, Science, Research and Tertiary Education*. Centre for the Study of Higher Education.https://www.ncsehe.edu.au/wp-content/uploads/2014/09/Critical-Interventions-Framework-20-August-2013.pdf

Pechenkina, E. (2015). Who needs support? Perceptions of institutional support by Indigenous Australian students at an Australian university. *UNESCO Observatory Multi-Disciplinary Journal in the Arts*, *4*(1), 1–21.

Penfold, C. (1996). Indigenous students' perceptions of factors contributing to successful law studies. *Legal Education Review*, 7(2), 155–191. http://www7.austlii.edu.au/cgi-bin/viewdoc/au/journals/LegEdRev/1996/7.html

Ryan, R. M. & Deci, E. L. (2000). Self-determination theory and the facilitation of intrinsic motivation, social development, and well-being. *American Psychologist*, *55*(1), 68–78. https://doi.apa.org/doi/10.1037/0003-066X.55.1.68

Stebleton, M. J., Soria, K. M. & Albecker, A. (2012). Integrating strength-based education into a first-year experience curriculum. *Journal of College and Character*, *13*(2), 1–8. https://doi.org/10.1515/jcc-2012-1877

Universities Australia. (2019). *Indigenous strategy first annual report*. https://www.universitiesaustralia.edu.au/wp-content/uploads/2019/06/20190304-Final-Indigenous-Strategy-Report-v2-2.pdf

Walker, R. (2000). *Indigenous performance in Western Australia universities: Reframing retention and success*. Commonwealth Department of Education, Training and Youth Affairs. https://www.voced.edu.au/content/ngv%3A61280#

Concluding remarks

An important aim of this book has been to expand and redirect the conversations about Indigenous student support in the higher education sector and to help shift the way those responsible for Indigenous students think about, discuss, and respond to the challenges they encounter in higher education. To do this, we have drawn some knowledge about higher education student success into the very centre of discussions. This is knowledge about the processes involved in academic learning, influences that can positively or negatively affect students' engagement and persistence, and the conditions necessary for Indigenous students to focus on learning how to learn and develop the capabilities they need to succeed. In drawing together this knowledge, we have elevated the criticality of the efforts students must exert and given credibility to the idea that their efforts are key to their success.

We then provided elements of a monitoring and tracking system for managing the cases of individual students, followed by the broader issues and services that require attention in any agenda that is focused on Indigenous students as learners who need support to develop the capacities to function successfully in academic study. In summary, seven key points need to be kept front of mind to drive any efforts for improving Indigenous student support and the daily work of staff.

The first is the importance of support staff *knowing all Indigenous students* and their goals, strengths, attributes, circumstances, challenges, educational progress, and needs from when they enter university and as these change during their studies. This requires strategies, systems, and processes for collecting, updating, and managing student information so it remains current and can be easily accessed in a timely manner.

The second is the importance of all support staff having *sound knowledge and understanding* of what is involved in higher education learning, the different demands of individual subjects and courses, the relevant university regulations and administrative procedures, the capabilities students need to succeed and eventually take control of their learning, and the effort required from students and support staff whose role it is to assist them to succeed.

The third key point is that *support must be individualised and in time* to improve students' outcomes and prevent negative outcomes concerning academic progress and socio-emotional wellbeing. This highlights the importance of efficient and in-time monitoring of student progress and the various factors affecting an individual's chances of success. Therefore, support staff need fit-for-purpose student

DOI: 10.4324/9781003326458-5

case management systems to help them serve the needs of students efficiently. This is particularly indicated for universities with large numbers of enabling and under-prepared Indigenous students, students with complex circumstances and needs, multi-campuses, and low outcomes. Further, the complex interplay between the many influences on individual students' success suggests that for most students, pastoral and academic support needs to be as integrated as possible and ongoing for the length of time it takes a student to develop the capabilities required to manage with minimal support.

It has been our experience that university student management systems are inadequate for the close management and monitoring of Indigenous student progress, but that externally sourced custom-designed systems are resisted. Therefore, support managers and senior Indigenous staff will need to have constructed compelling arguments for having such a system and be well informed about the security of information within them and how they access information from university systems. It took three years of development and some hard bargaining before our current university agreed to a trial. However, the benefits of improved student outcomes have led to full acceptance of the system we now use.

The fourth key point is that support staff need a *reflective practice* for considering what aspects of their support practices work well and what aspects need review, rethinking, changes, or adjustments. This implies the need for an annual or semester-based plan, review, evaluation, and adjustment cycle.

Fifth, Indigenous student support should be *recognised as a professional area of practice*, where students' needs are the priority and staff adhere to professional ethics, without letting go of the Indigenous values and practices that increase the effectiveness of their work or without retaining those that do not benefit students. All staff who support Indigenous students should receive the professional development required to operate effectively, efficiently, and ethically.

Sixth, *universities have a responsibility* and a role in ensuring that Indigenous student support staff have the infrastructure and mechanisms for accessing, collecting, and analysing the data they need to provide effective, efficient, and prompt support to all Indigenous students. Student support managers have a responsibility to assist their staff to make the best use of this infrastructure. These mechanisms must also manage information that is not collected by universities but relates to tracking Indigenous students and staff responses and support interventions.

Seventh, efforts to improve support services are unlikely to succeed unless there is a *well-devised plan* to guide change. Indigenous student support is complex and requires investment and commitment on the part of universities, but, most importantly, it requires a plan that support managers and staff can implement. Managers and staff must know (or should know) their Indigenous students and need to understand the 'why, what and how' of their support work. Support staff need to follow a long-term plan that suits the local situation, takes an educationally informed approach, is implemented over time, and is continuously evaluated and adjusted every year if necessary. Calls for change and rhetorical statements of commitment or good intentions achieve little if there is no considered and sustainable action plan.

Stripped to its essentials, the shift in thinking we have been unfolding in this book emphasises and connects the links between Indigenous student outcomes,

Indigenous students' capacity levels, staff knowledge about the capabilities and study conditions students need for successful higher education learning, efforts Indigenous students must make to achieve academic learning successes, and what student support managers and staff need to understand, consider, and act upon to support all Indigenous students who require assistance to develop the capabilities they need to succeed. This web of connections is important—hopefully, there will be fewer holes for students to fall through where they are beyond the focus of the staff responsible for providing support.

What Indigenous student support staff do and how they do it matters for Indigenous students and their immediate and future outcomes. The Indigenous student support sector needs their challenges to be acknowledged and requires support to improve their practices. Hopefully, this book will redirect how we discuss Indigenous student support and where it sits within Indigenous higher education and university priorities.

Index

For Product Safety Concerns and Information please contact our EU
representative GPSR@taylorandfrancis.com
Taylor & Francis Verlag GmbH, Kaufingerstraße 24, 80331 München, Germany

9 781032 353463